Fantastic Art And The Creative Process   Volume 2

ViSion
ILLUSTRATED

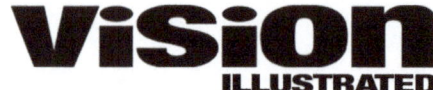

Fantastic Art And The Creative Process

Volume 2

www.visionillustrated.com

info@visionillustrated.com

Vision Illustrated, TM and Copyright © 2018 Hugo Bravo.
All rights reserved. All Images featured in this book are ©2018 to their respective artists/copyright holders unless otherwise specified.

No part of this book may be reproduced, stored, or transmitted by any means—whether auditory, graphic, mechanical, or electronic—without written permission of both publisher and author, except in the case of brief excerpts used in critical articles and reviews.
Unauthorized reproduction of any part of this work is illegal and is punishable by law.

Because of the dynamic nature of the Internet, any web addresses or links contained in this book may have changed since publication and may no longer be valid. The views expressed in this work are solely those of the author and do not necessarily reflect the views of the publisher, and the publisher hereby disclaims any responsibility for them.

Cover and book design by Hugo Bravo

First Printing: 2018

ISBN: 9781726892995

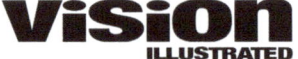

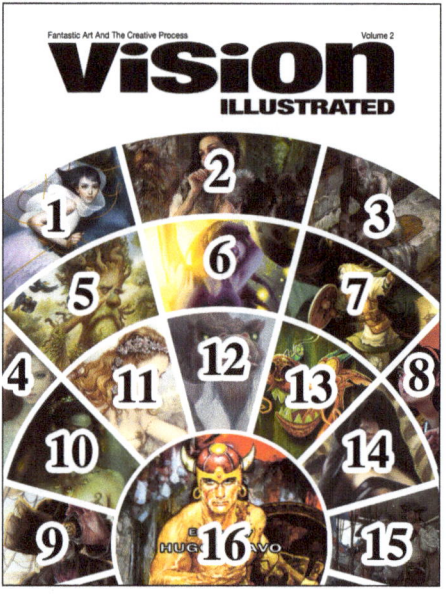

Cover Art:

1. Tran Nguyen
2. Alessandra Pisano
3. Donato Giancola
4. Annie Stegg
5. Justin Gerard
6. Rob Rey
7. Mike Sass
8. Carly Mazur
9. Lindsey Look
10. Patrick Jones
11. Arantza Sestayo
12. Allen Douglas
13. Jeff Miracola
14. Kelley Hensing
15. Don Maitz
16. Sanjulian

Fantastic Art And The Creative Process

Volume 2

ViSion
ILLUSTRATED

Edited by
HUGO BRAVO

art by JORGE FARFÁN

vision ILLUSTRATED
Contributing Artists

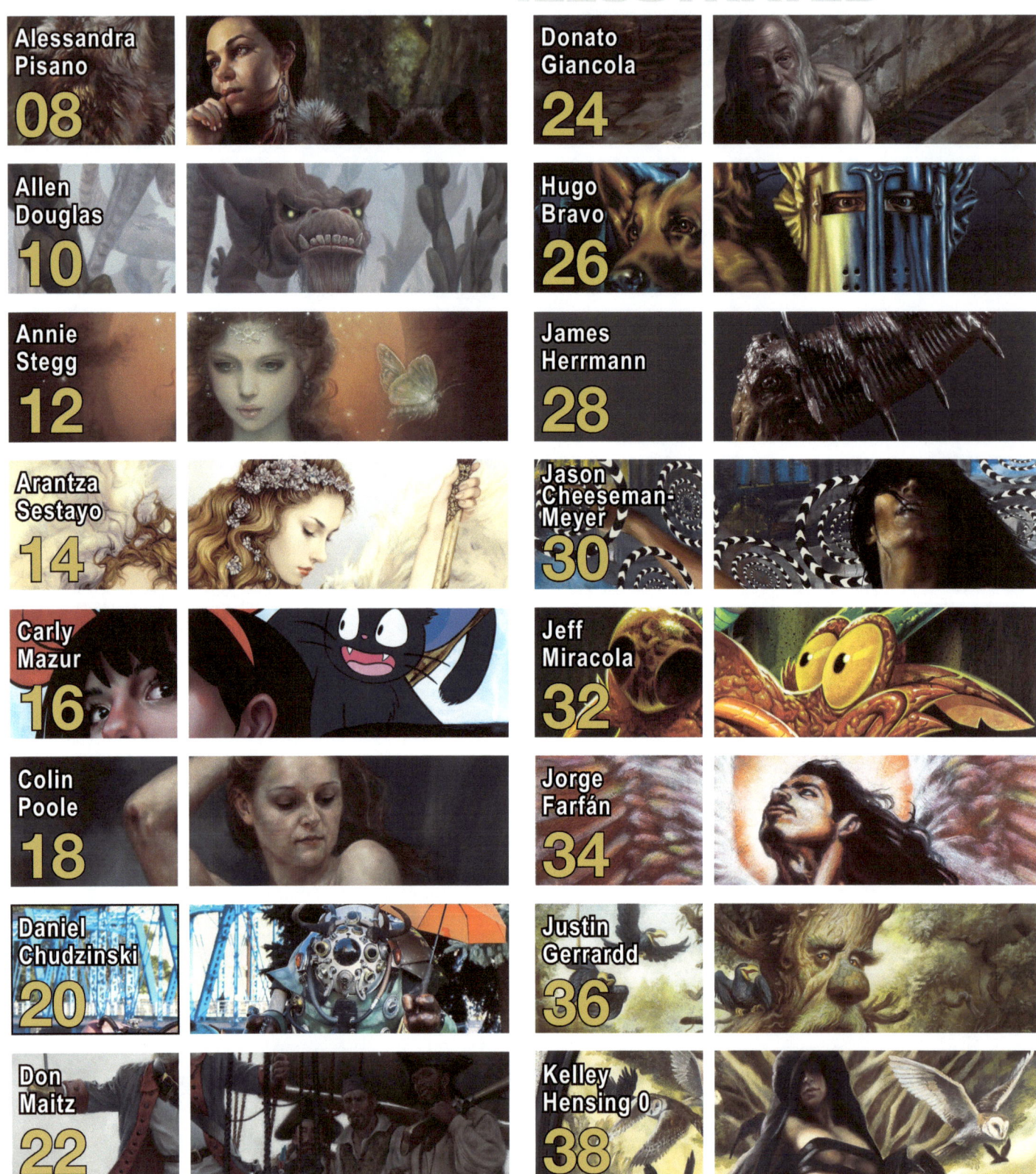

- Alessandra Pisano — 08
- Allen Douglas — 10
- Annie Stegg — 12
- Arantza Sestayo — 14
- Carly Mazur — 16
- Colin Poole — 18
- Daniel Chudzinski — 20
- Don Maitz — 22
- Donato Giancola — 24
- Hugo Bravo — 26
- James Herrmann — 28
- Jason Cheeseman-Meyer — 30
- Jeff Miracola — 32
- Jorge Farfán — 34
- Justin Gerrardd — 36
- Kelley Hensing 0 — 38

Vision Illustrated
Contributing Artists

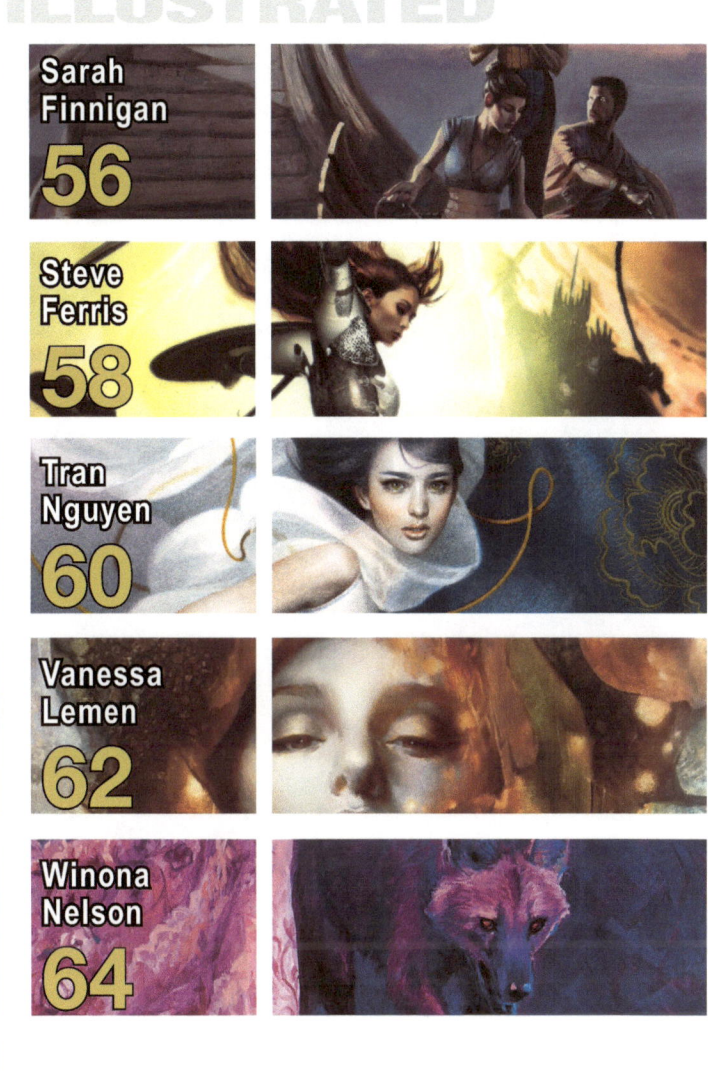

- Kristine & Colin Poole — 40 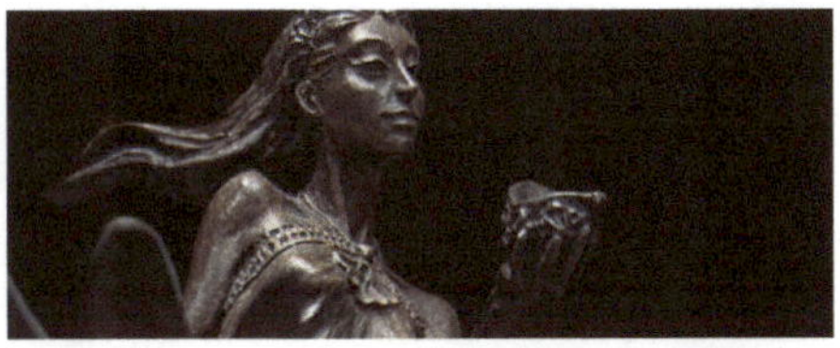
- Linda Adair — 42 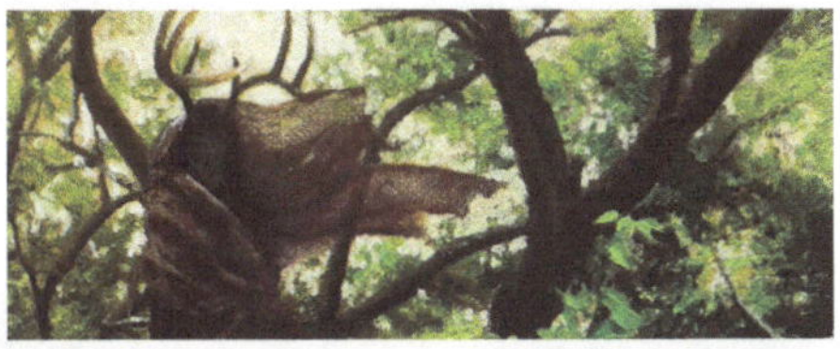
- Lindsey Look — 44 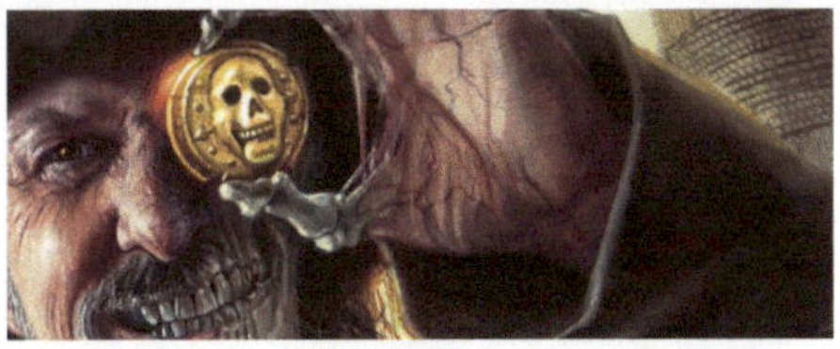
- Mike Sass — 46 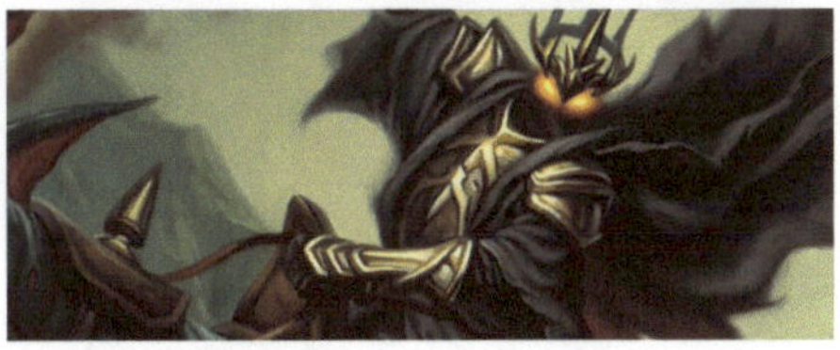
- Patrick Jones — 48 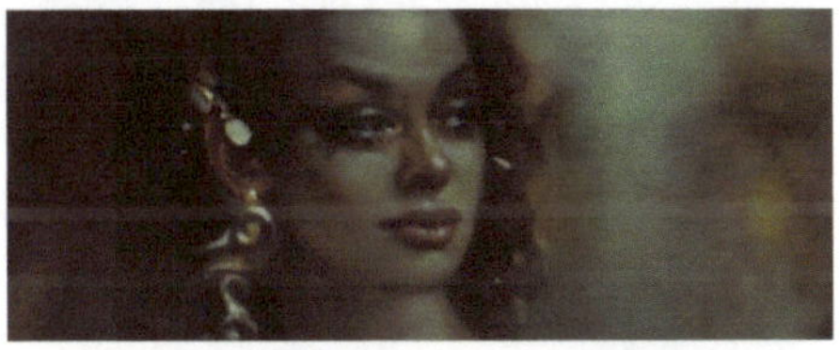
- Rob Rey — 50 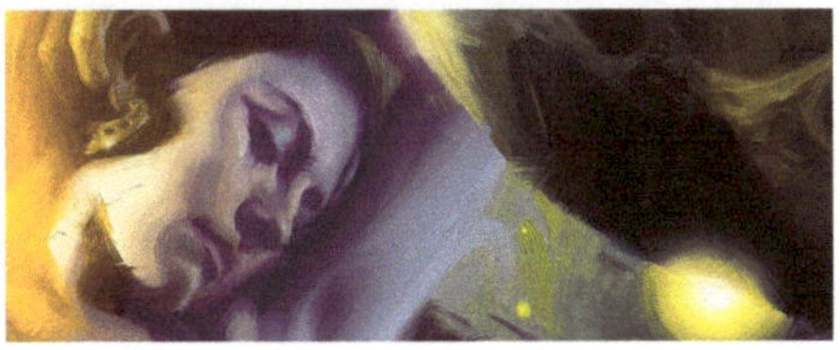
- Ruth Sanderson — 52 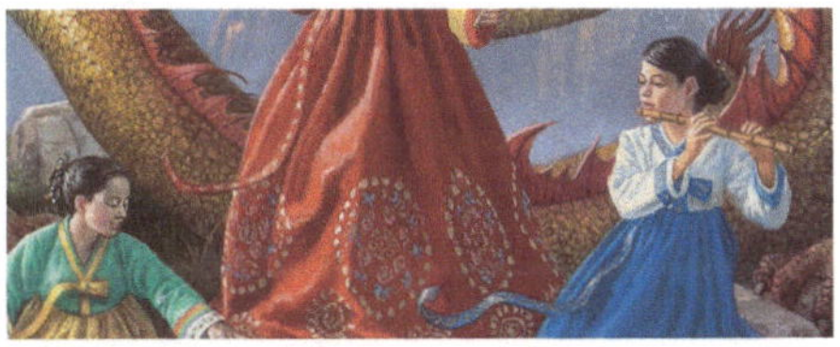
- Sanjulian — 54 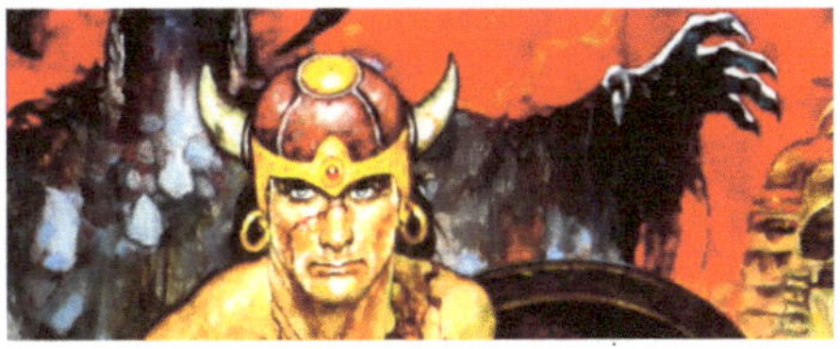
- Sarah Finnigan — 56
- Steve Ferris — 58
- Tran Nguyen — 60
- Vanessa Lemen — 62
- Winona Nelson — 64

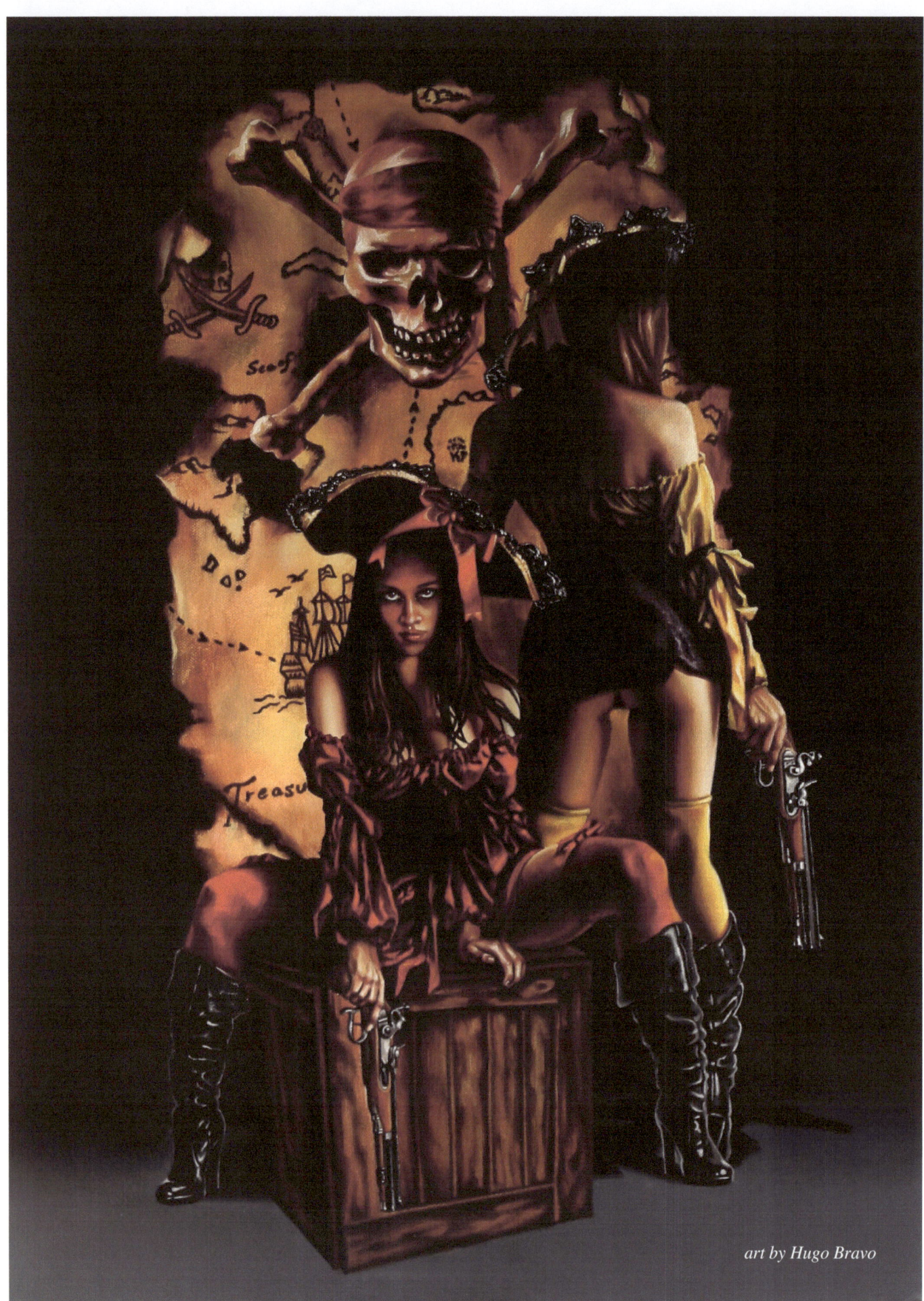
art by Hugo Bravo

Forward

Welcome to the 2nd volume of Vision Illustrated!

In this edition you will find more than 200 images representing the creative process of today's top illustrators of Fantastic Art. As with volume one of Vision Illustrated, each artists gets two full pages to display their artwork and creative process. We believe this format allows for the best image representation without restrictions on image size. If you find any art within Vision Illustrated of interest to you, each artist page will provide you with the contact information for the artist as well. It is a privilege and an honor to showcase these artists and their works of art. Thank you to all the artists who have contributed to Vision Illustrated Volume 2!

Many of the artists found in this volume of Vision Illustrated gather to exhibit their work at an annual event called IlluxCon (IX). For over a decade IX has been and continues to be the world's leading organization dedicated to contemporary imaginative realism. This event is the opportunity for artists, students, collectors and art fans to get up close and personal with these and many other outstanding artists. Along with their online gallery IXGallery.com, IX is your way to discover Fantastic Art.

Starting with this volume we now include sculptors in our showcase. We welcome and are grateful for the contributions of sculptors Daniel Chudzinski, James Herrmann, Kristine & Colin Poole. Working in a variety of mediums and each having a unique creative process, Vision Illustrated puts you in the studio with the sculptor and shows you how these three dimensional works are created.

I wish to thank you for your interest and support of Vision Illustrated. The idea of this book is to celebrate the world of Fantastic Art while giving something extra to the reader. We call this "an insight into the creative process" of each artist in our showcase. Through multiple images, some of which have never been published, each artist invites you to their studio to witness the creation of Fantastic Art.

All the best,

Hugo Bravo

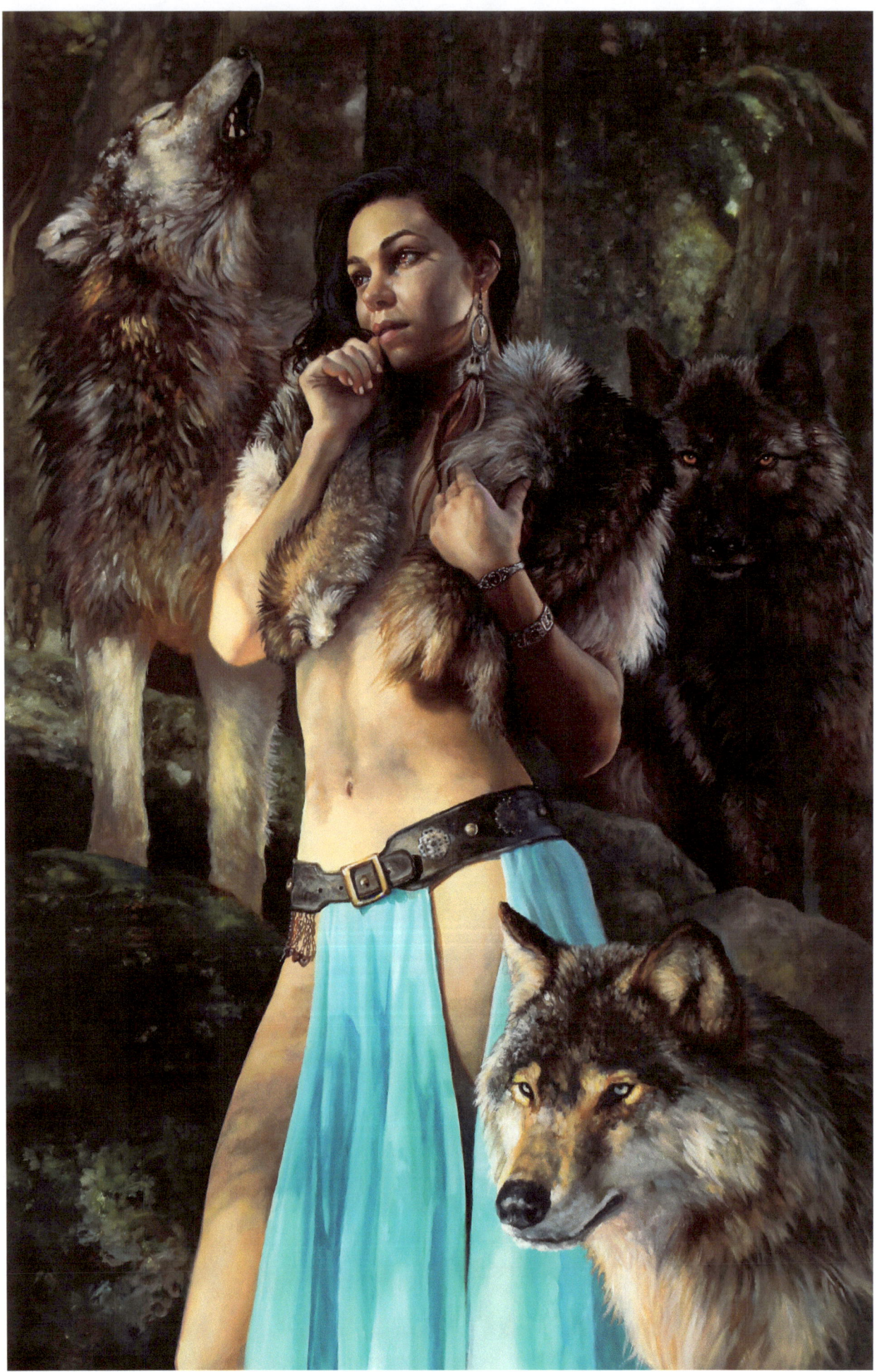

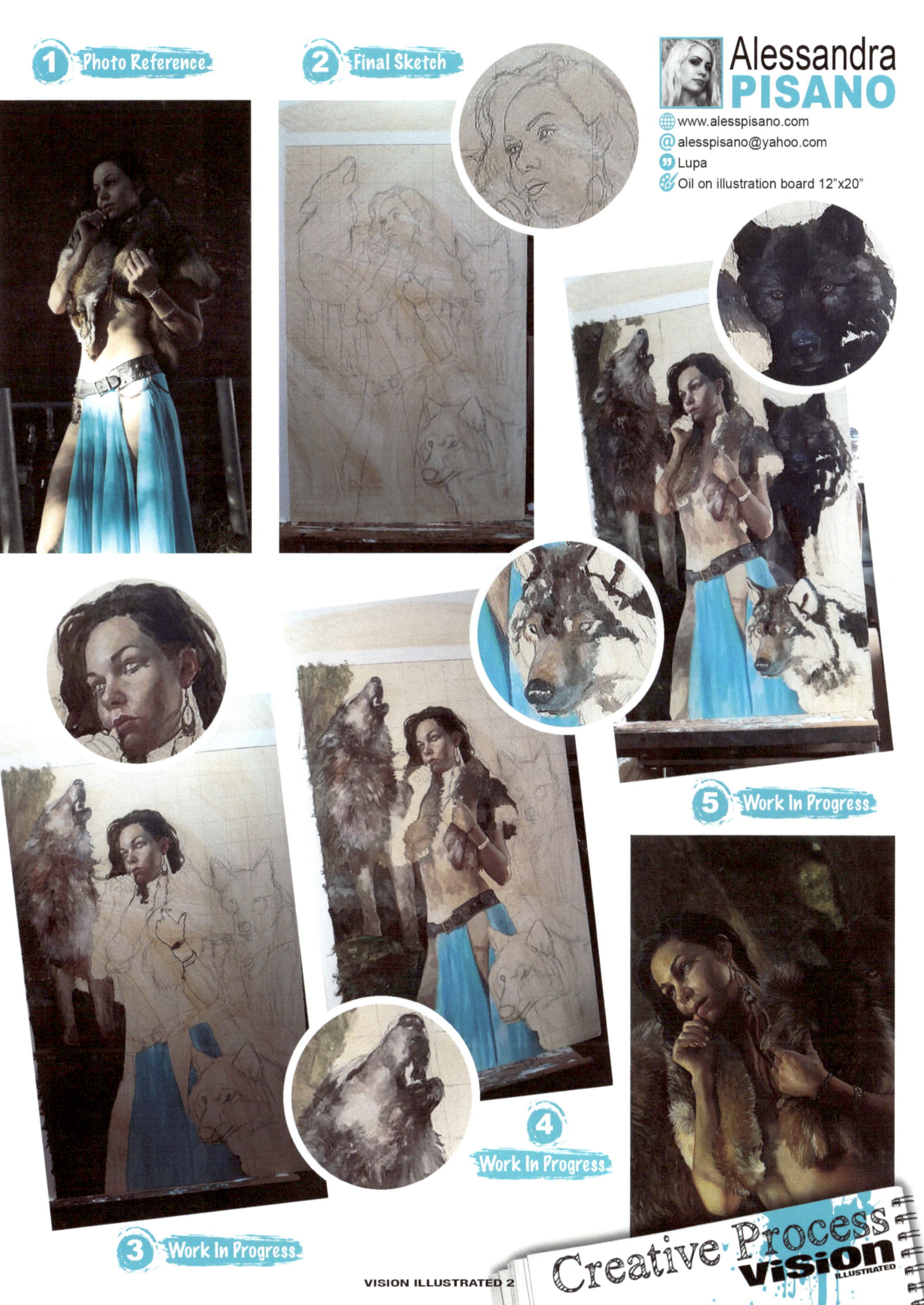

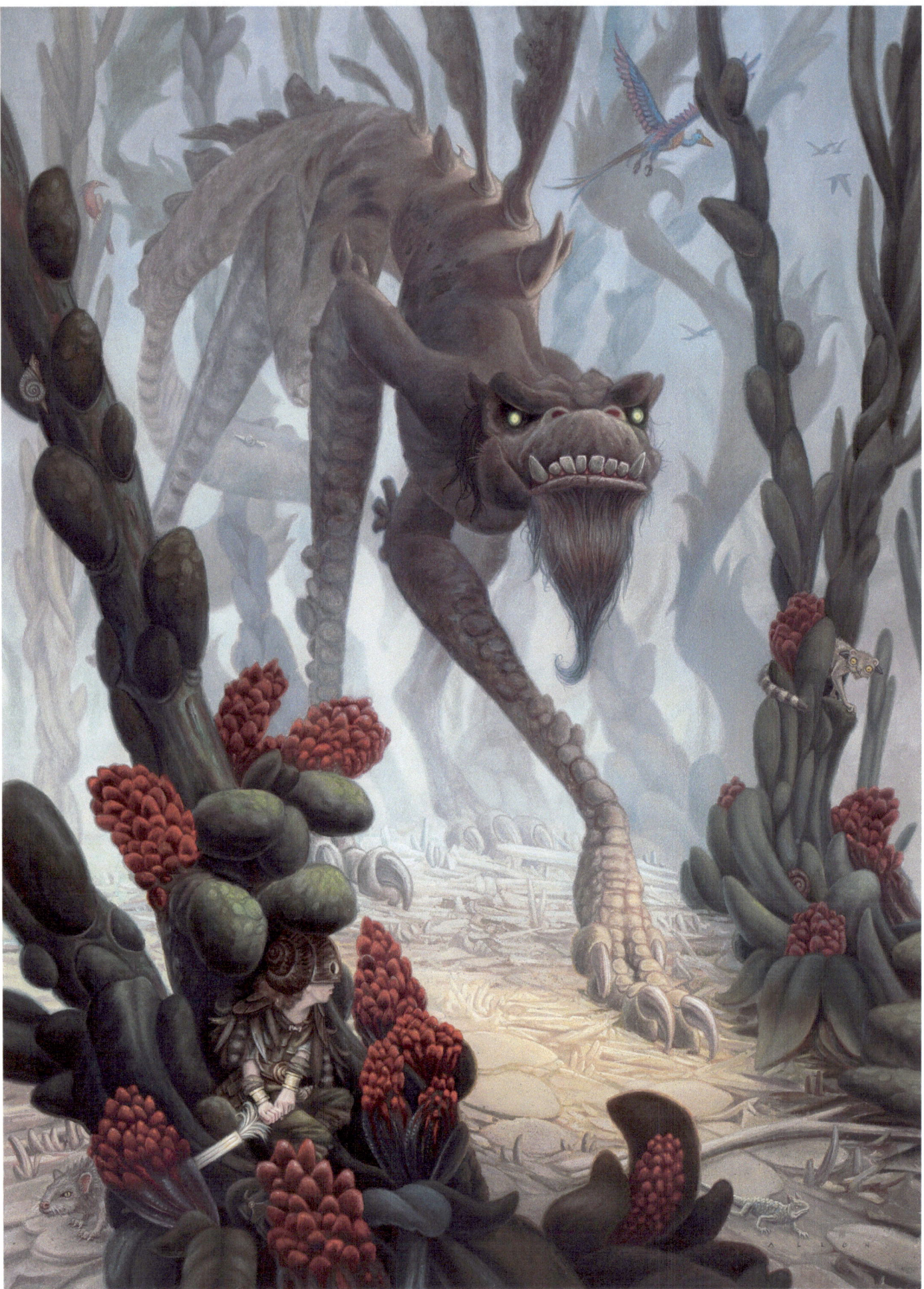

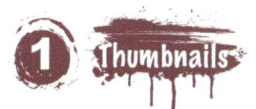
1 Thumbnails

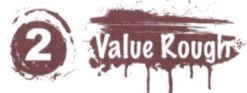
2 Value Rough

Allen DOUGLAS

🌐 www.cryptidvisions.com
✉ allen@cryptidvisions.com
💬 The Jabberwock
🖌 Oil on panel 18"X24"

3 Color Rough

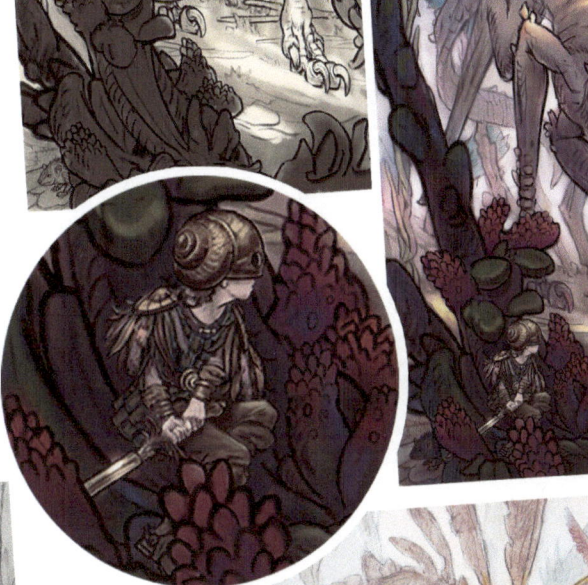

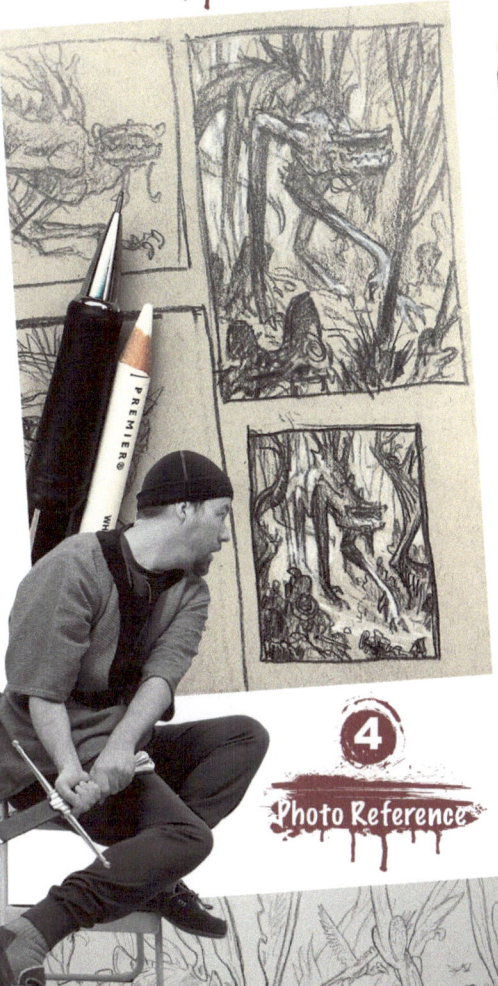

4 Photo Reference

5 Final Sketch

6 Underpainting

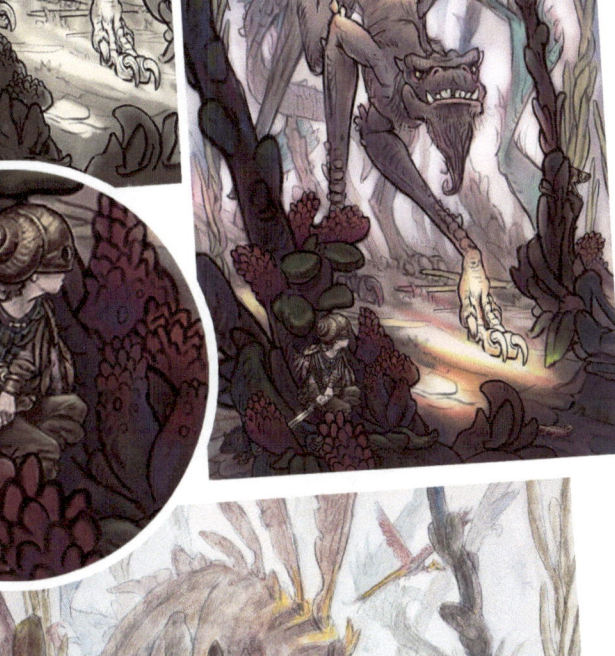

VISION ILLUSTRATED 2

Creative Process

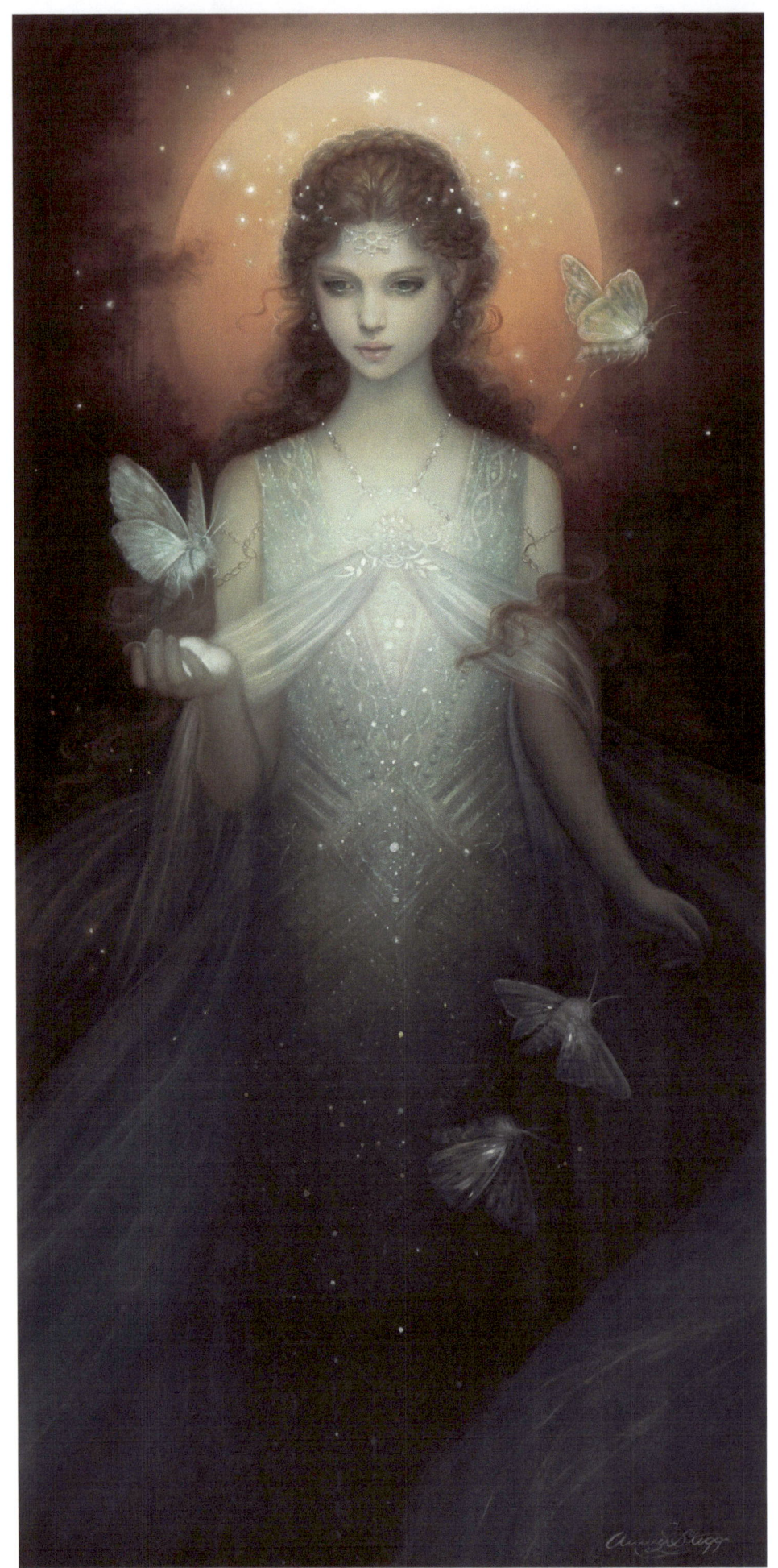

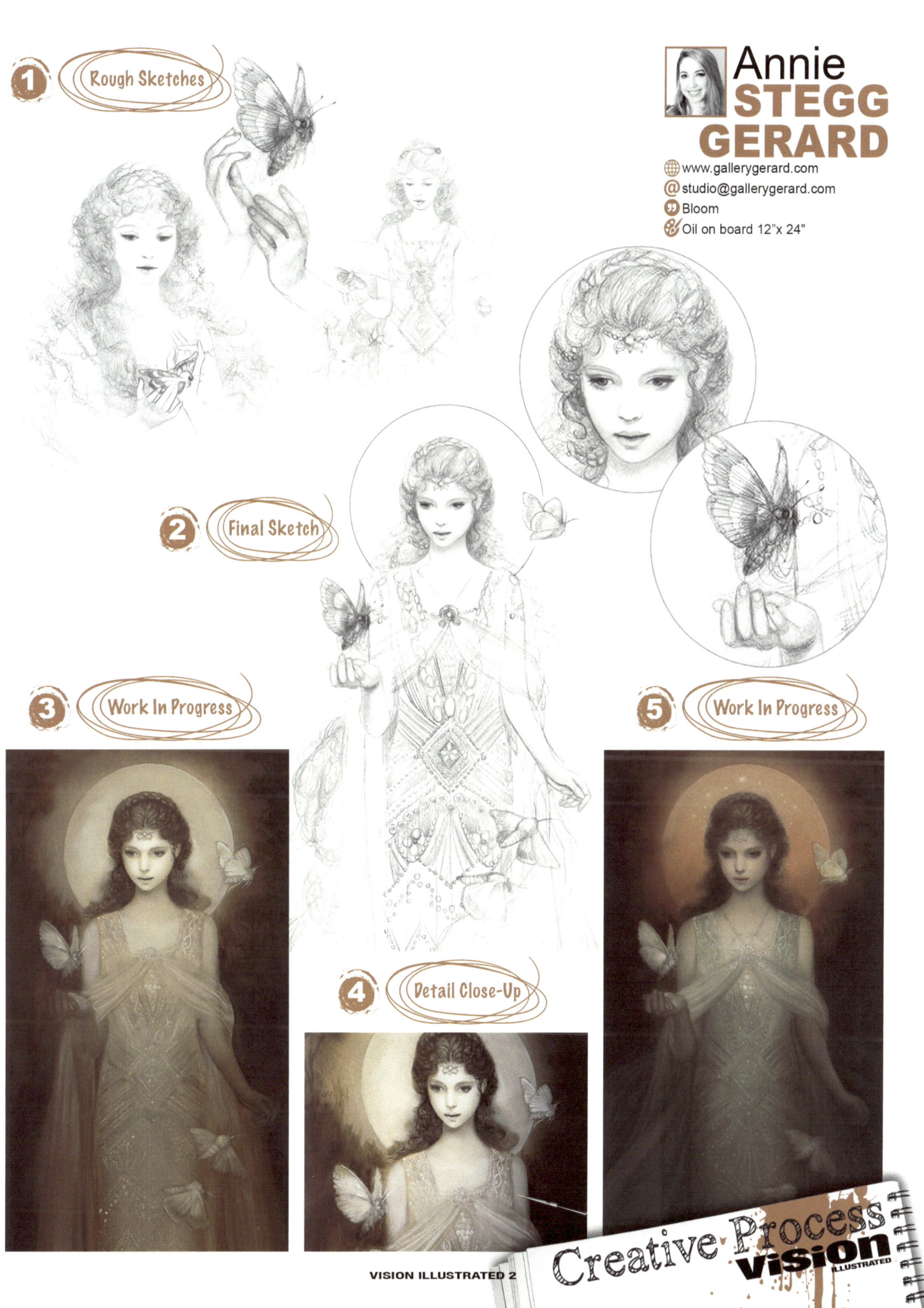

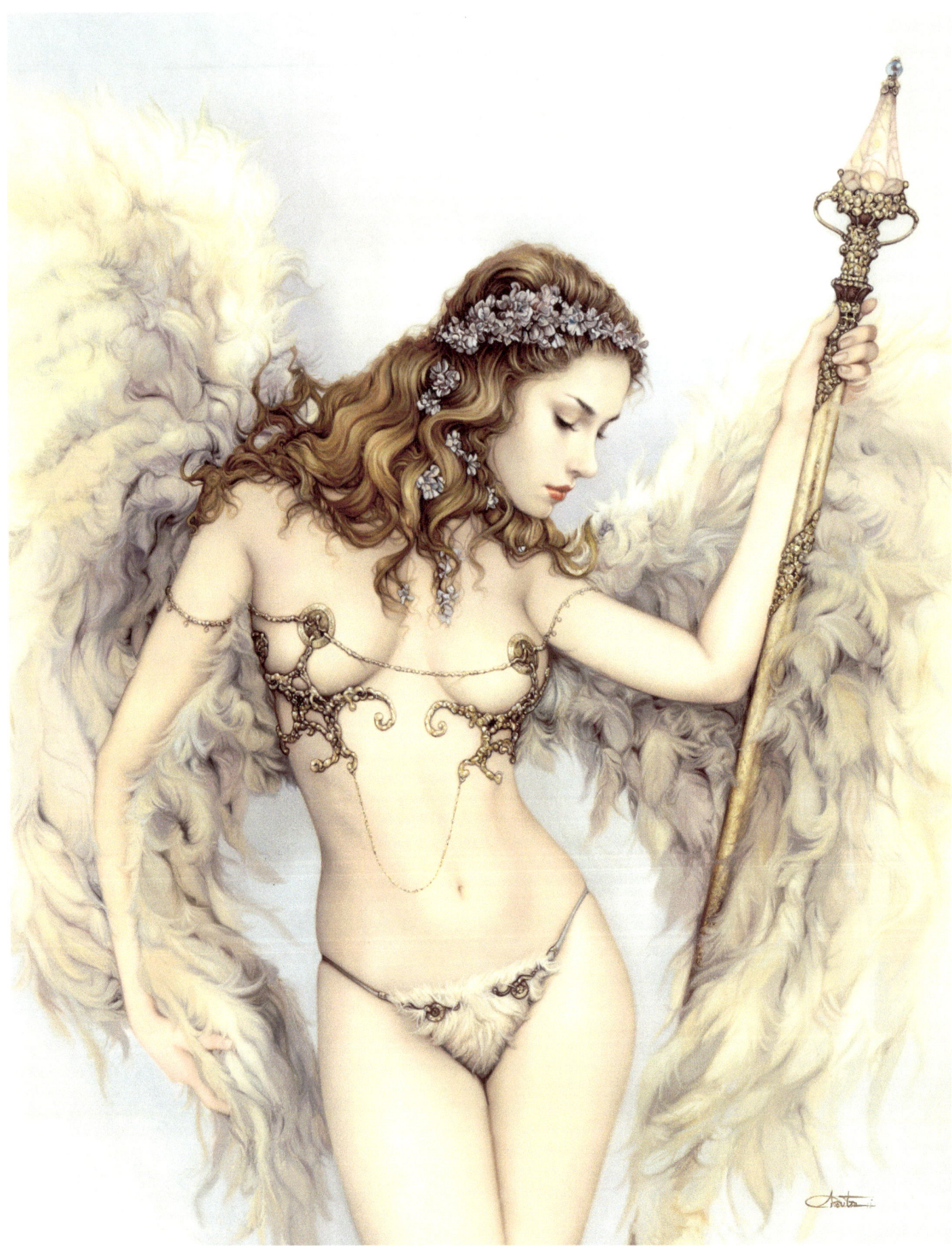

1 Thumbnail Sketch

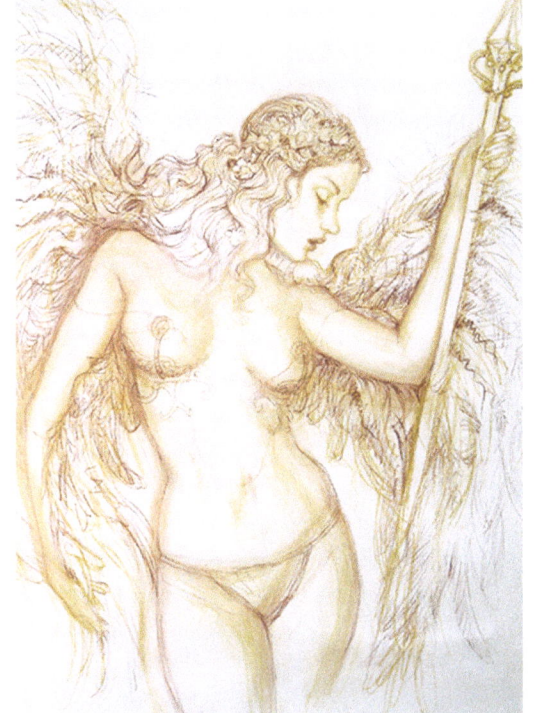

2 Final Sketch

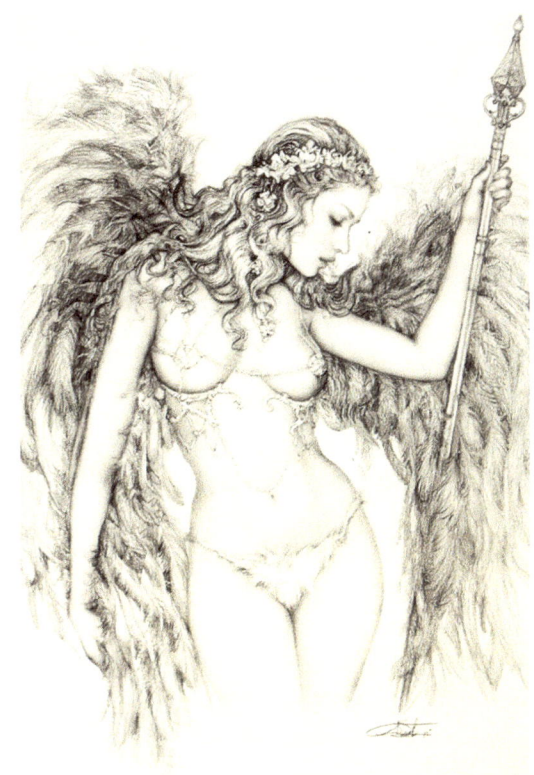

3 Detail Close Ups

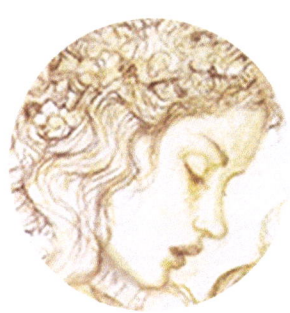
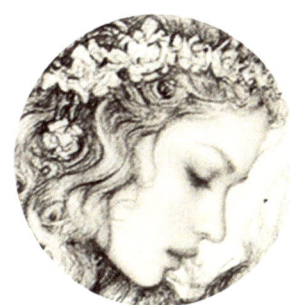
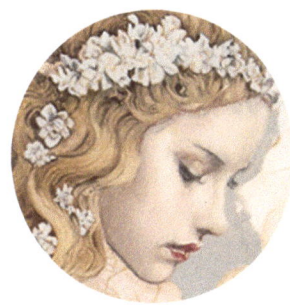
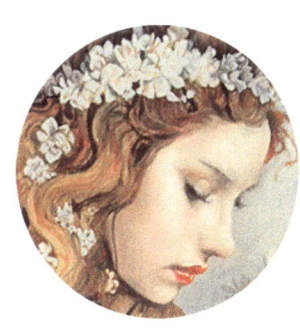

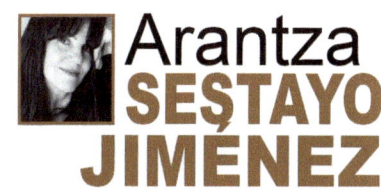
Arantza
SESTAYO
JIMENEZ

🌐 www.arantzasestayo.com
@ arantzasestayo@gmail.com
🔗 Margella
🎨 Oil on canvas 24"x30"

4 Work In Progress

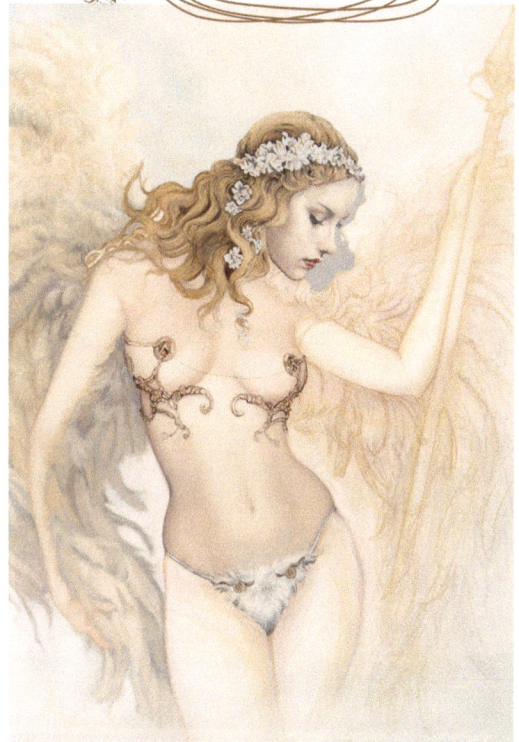

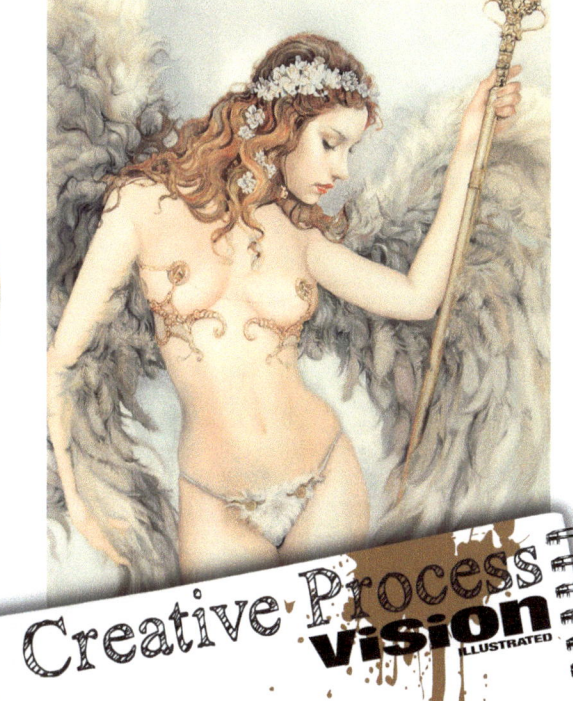

Creative Process

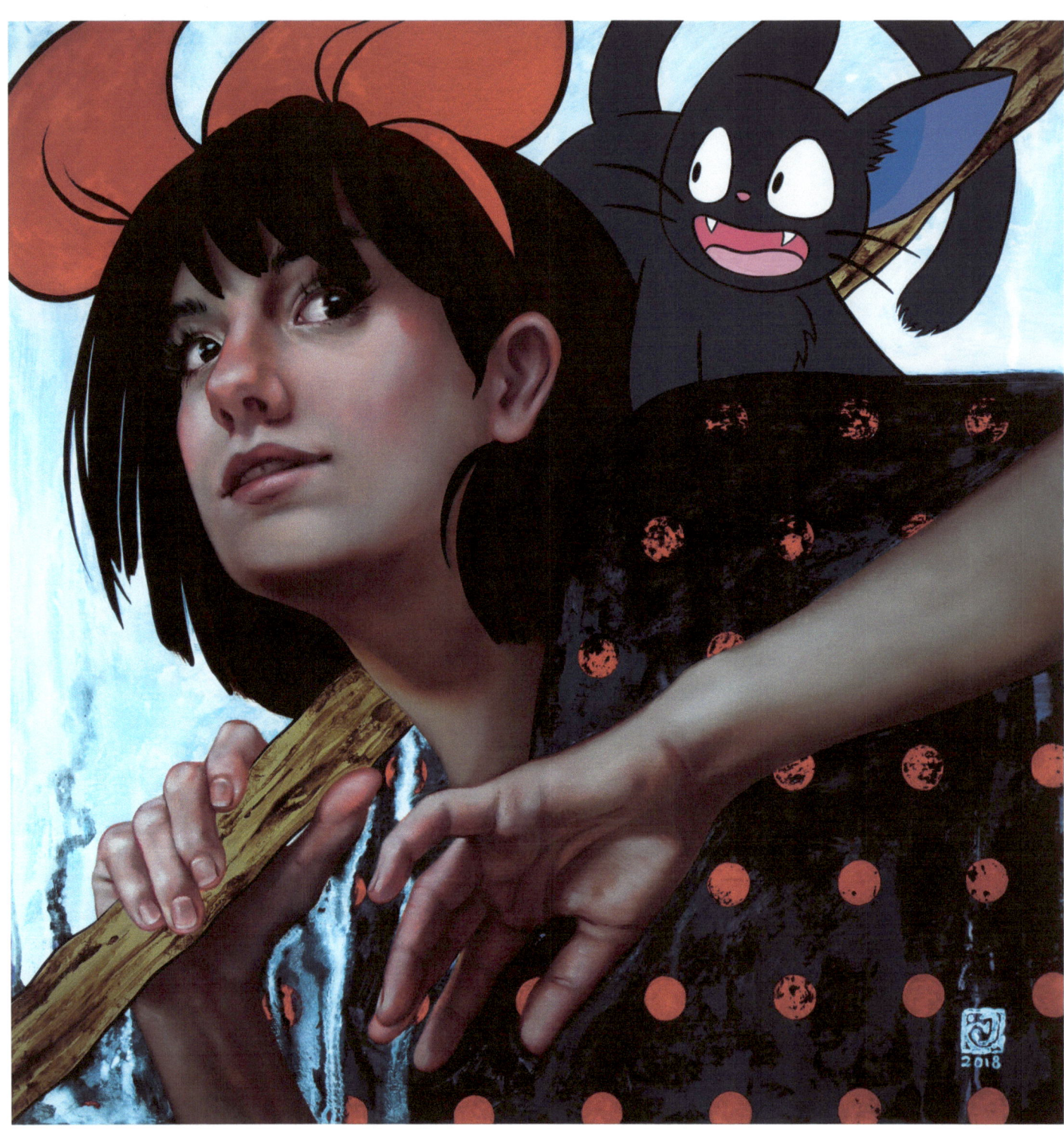

1. Thumbnail Sketches

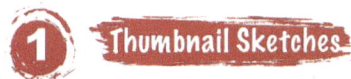
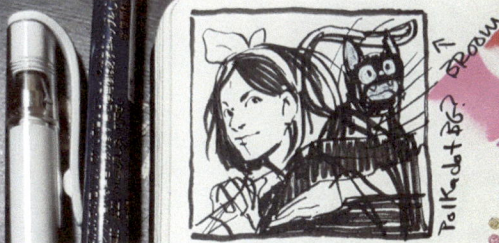
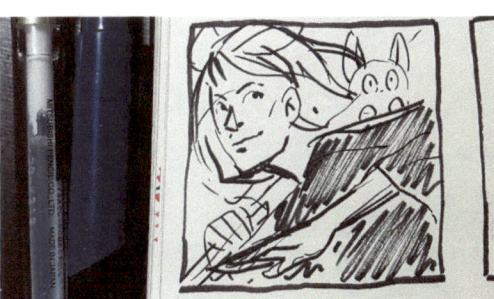

2. Photo Reference

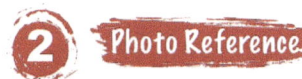
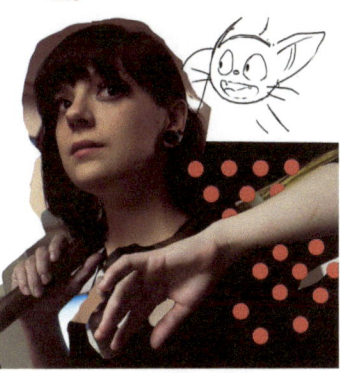

4. Work In Progress

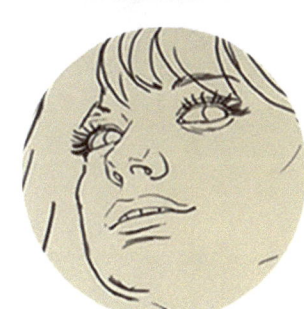
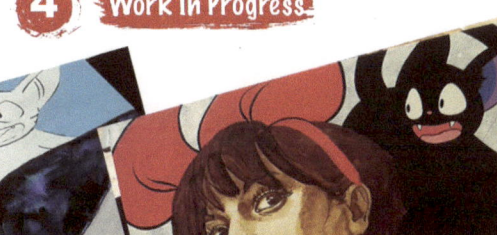
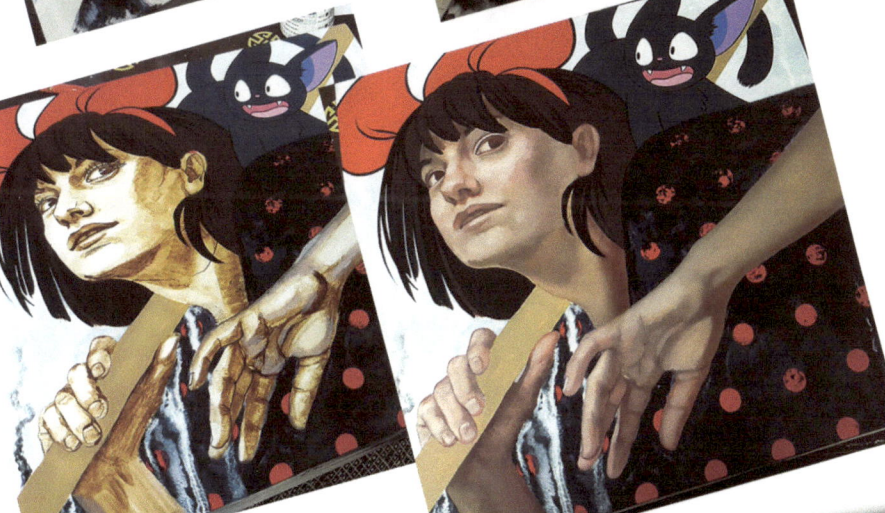

Carly JANINE MAZUR

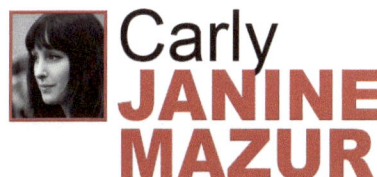

- www.carlyjanine.com
- Kiki's Delivery Service
- Oil & Acrylic on cradled board 12"x 12"

3. Final Sketch

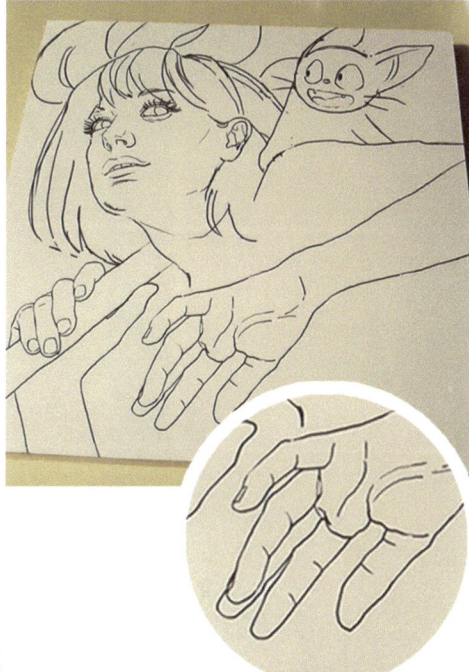

5. Detail Close Up

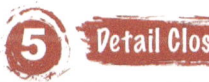
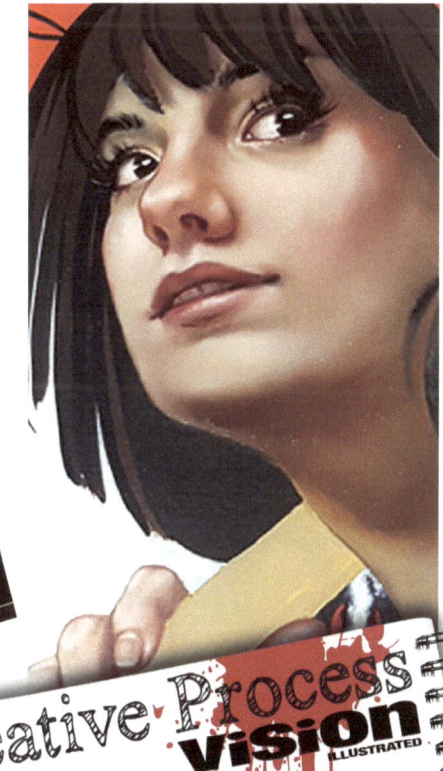

Creative Process

VISION ILLUSTRATED 2

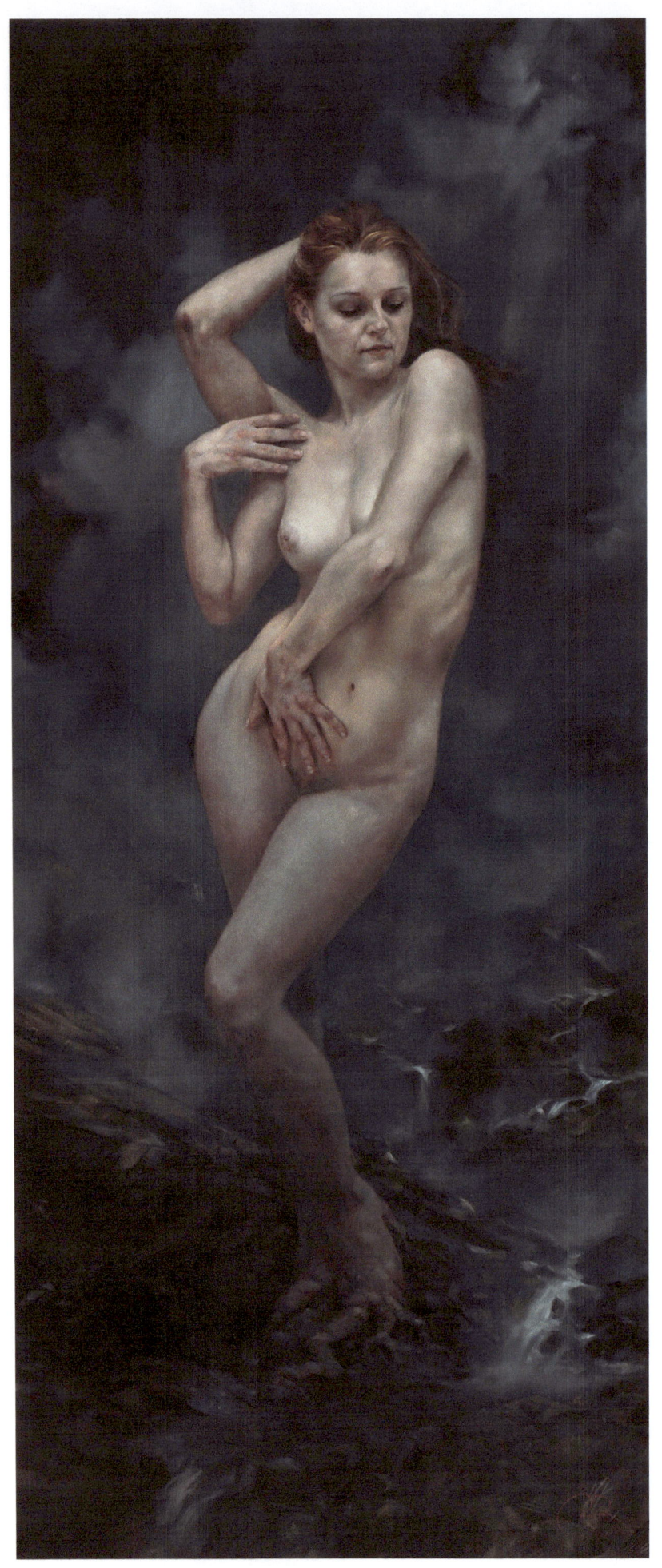

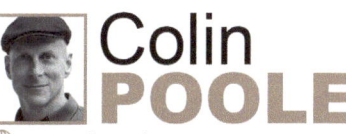

Colin POOLE

🌐 www.colinpoole.com
@ colin@colinpoole.com
📞 800-808-5005
💬 The Valley of Mists
🎨 Oil on linen 26"x 60"

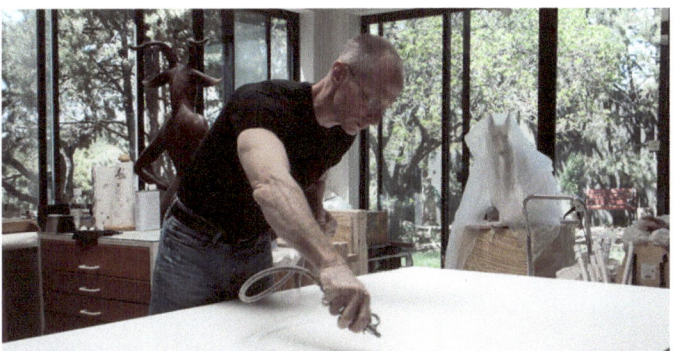

1 Prepping Canvas

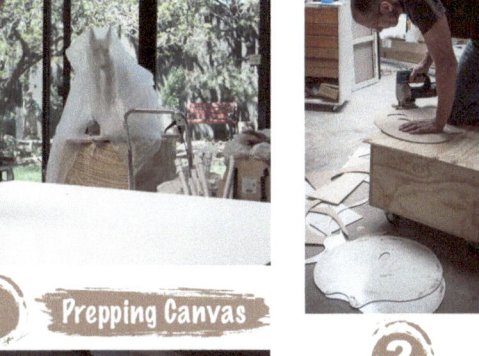

2 Cutting custom palettes

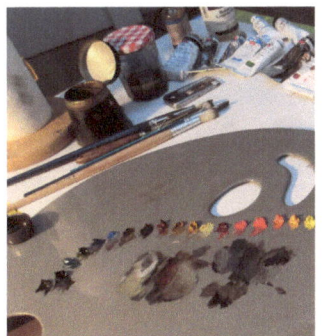
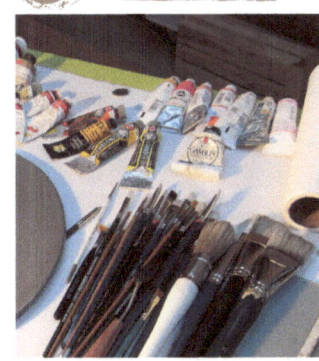
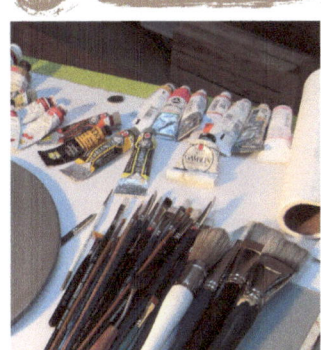
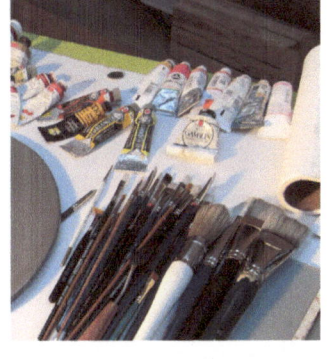

3 Underpainting with rag and brush

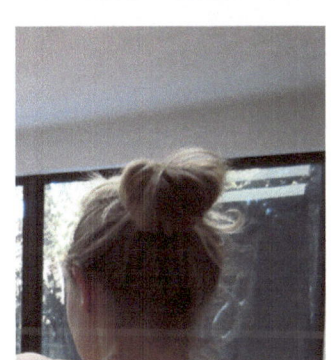

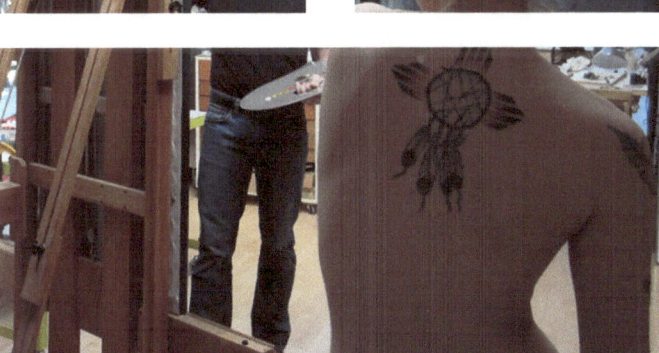

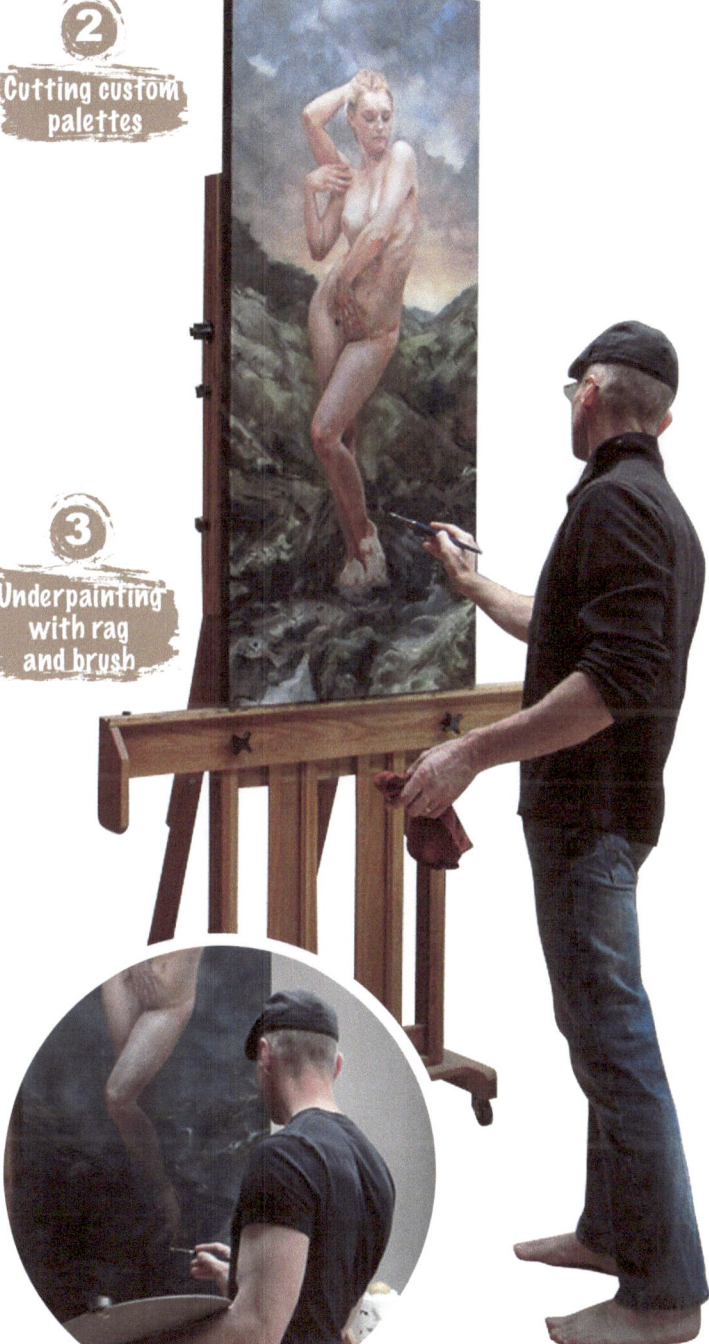

4 Changing the background

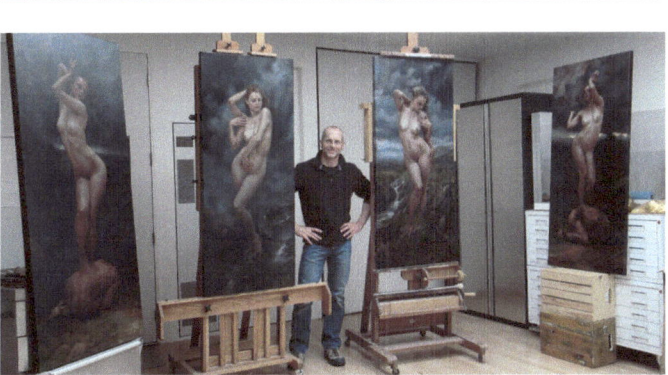

6 The series

VISION ILLUSTRATED 2

Creative Process
VISION ILLUSTRATED

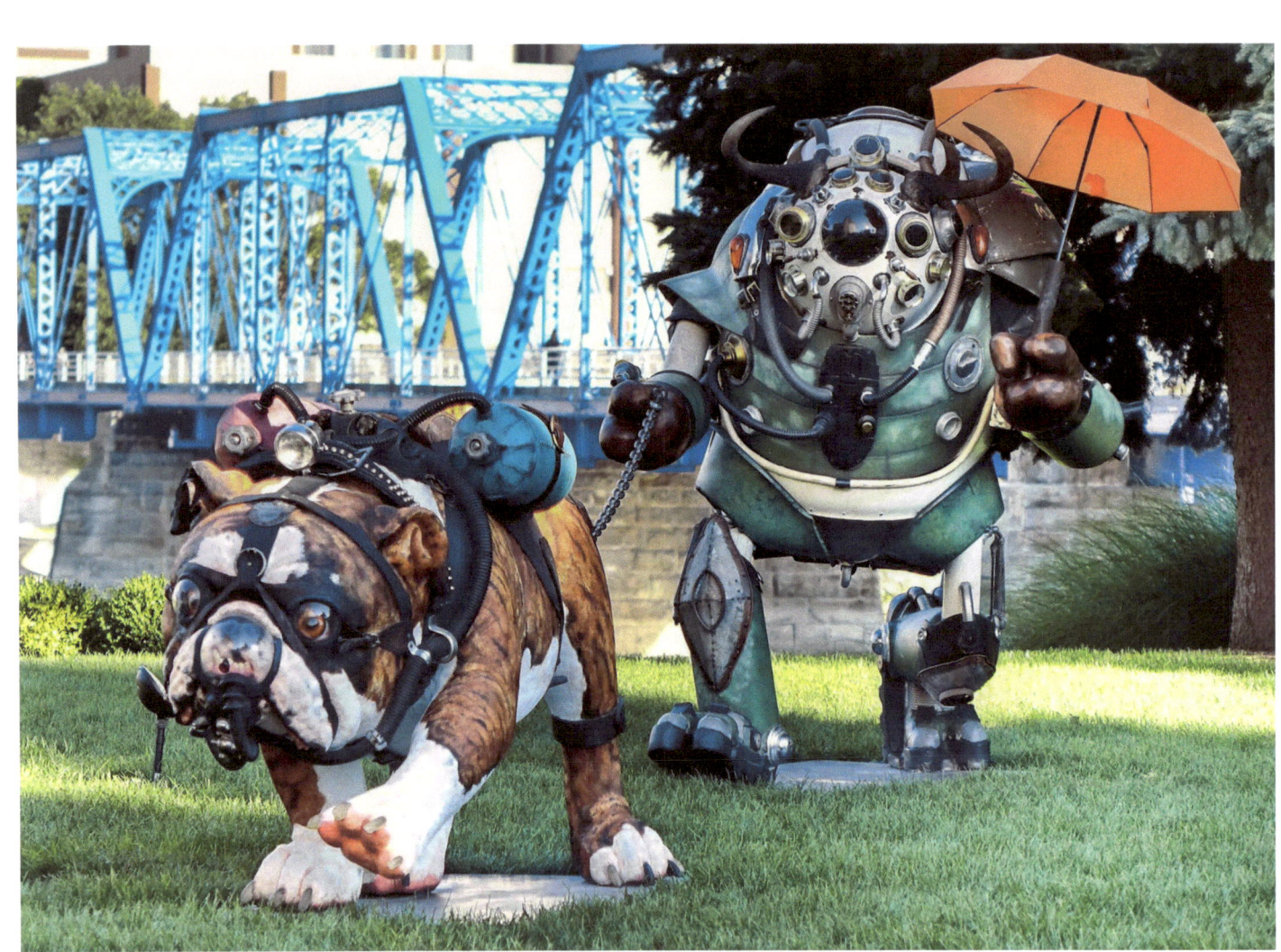

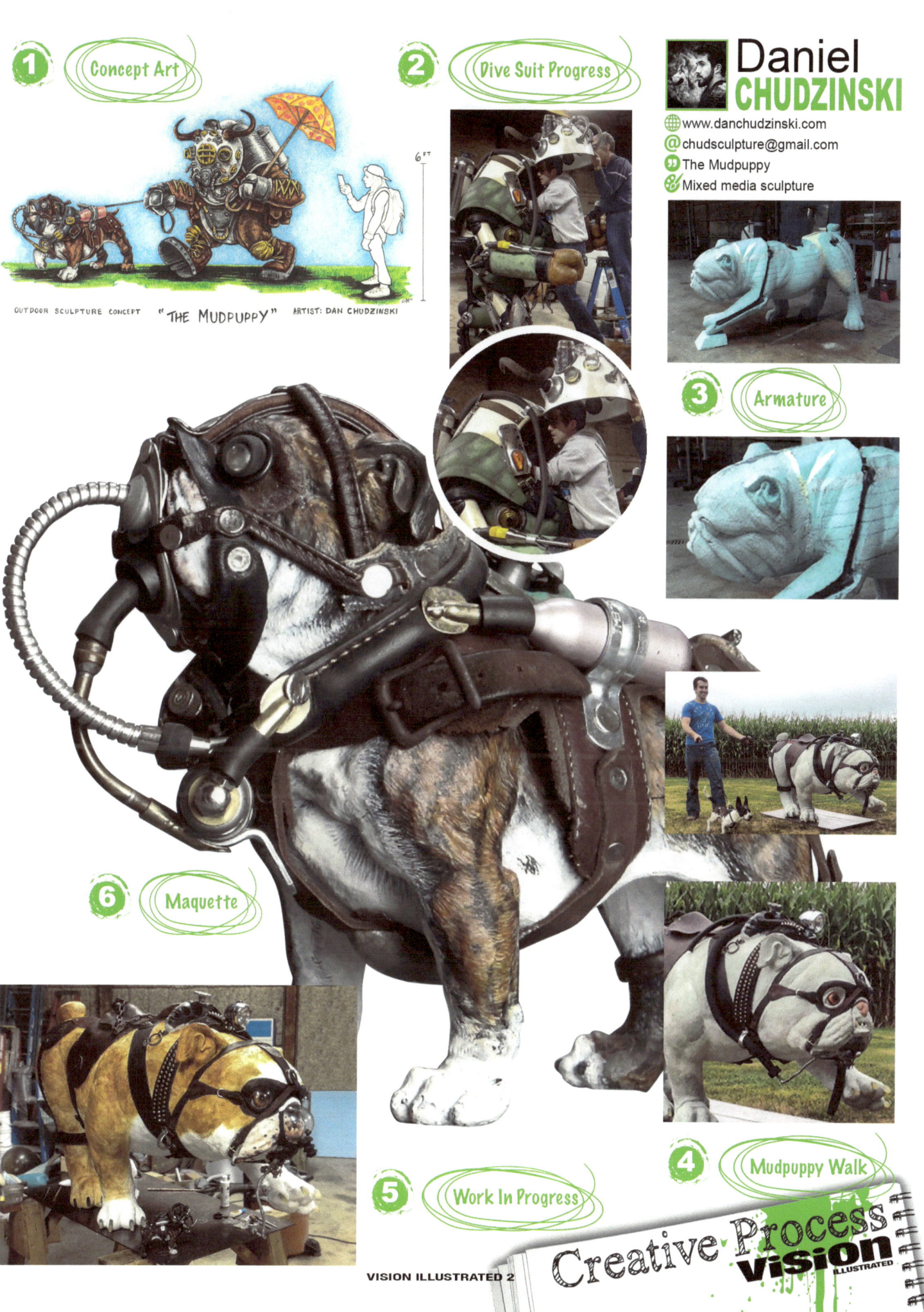

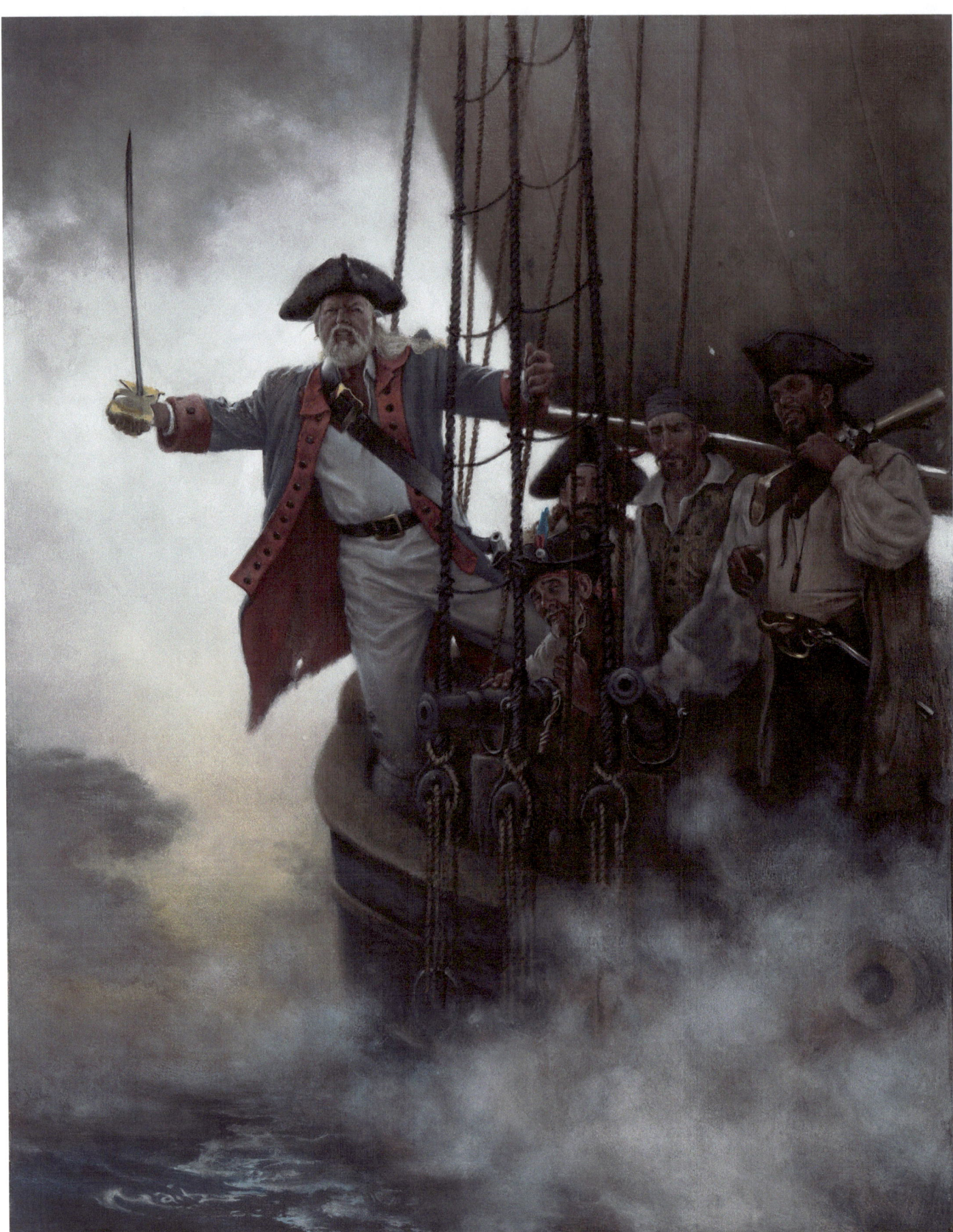

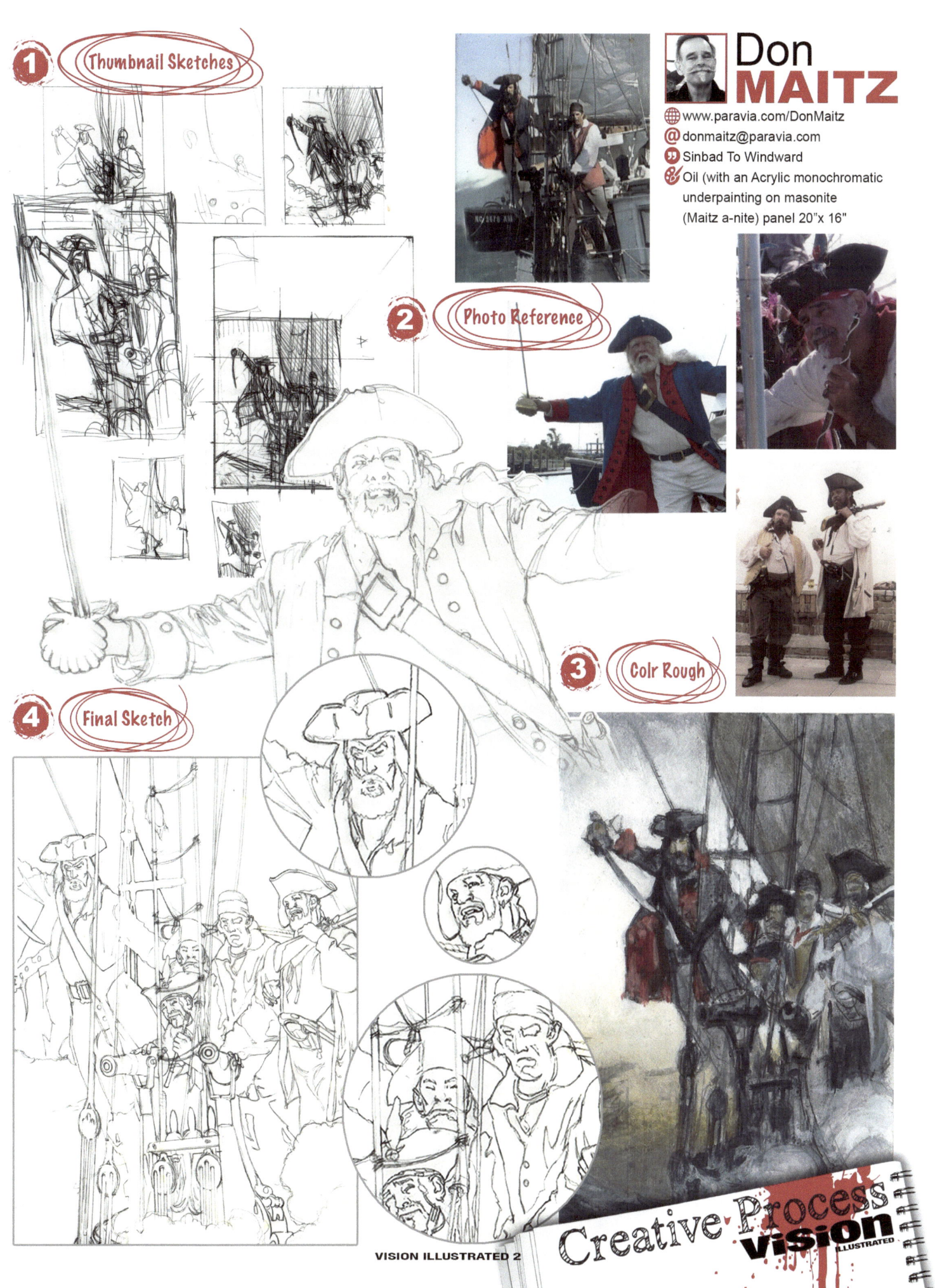

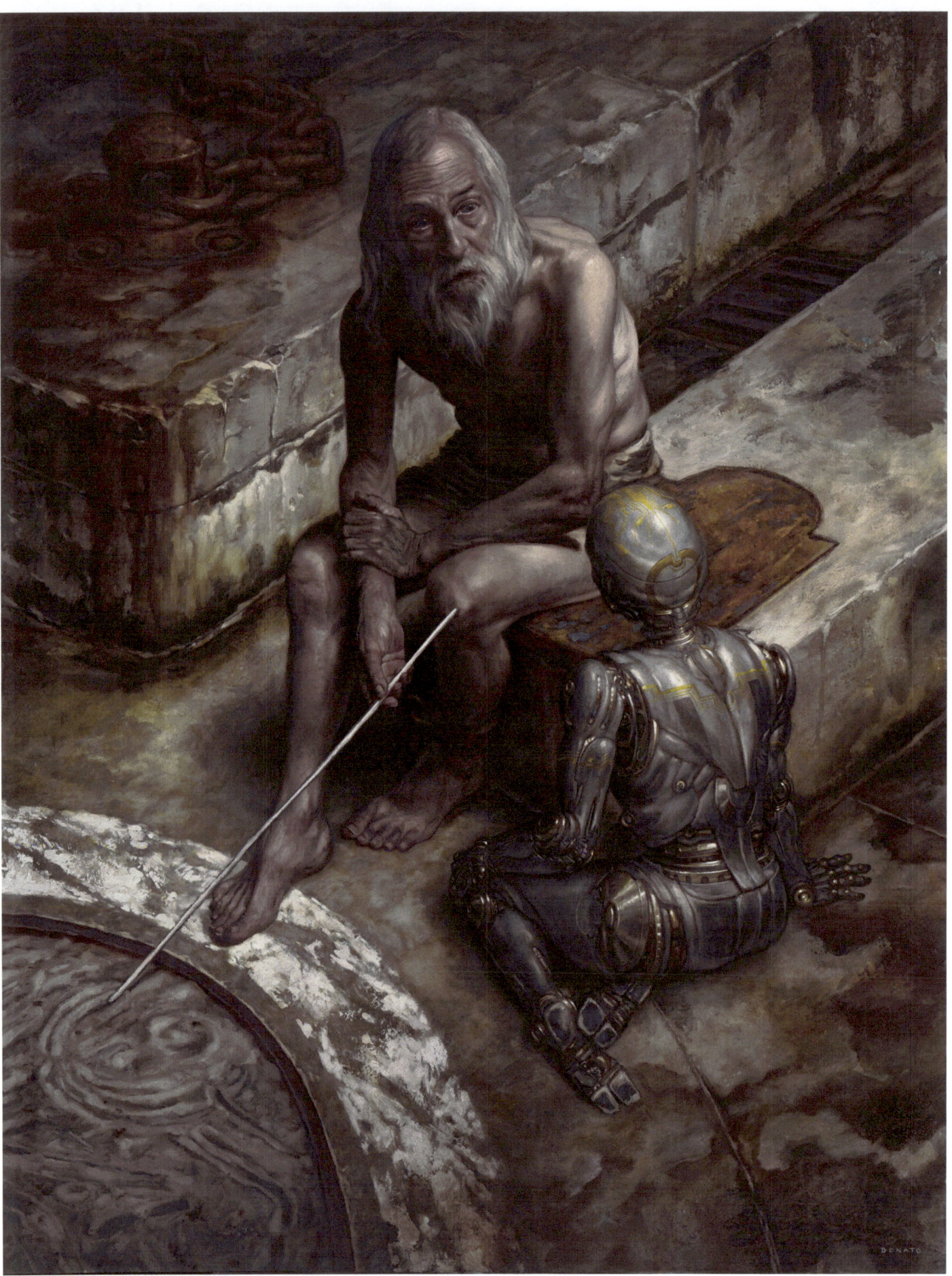

① **Thumbnail Sketches**

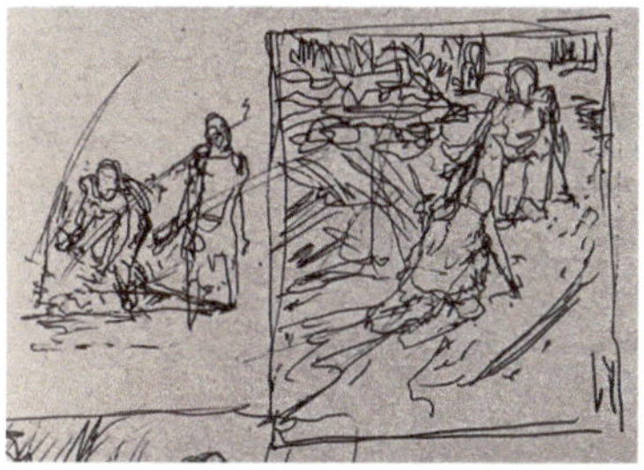

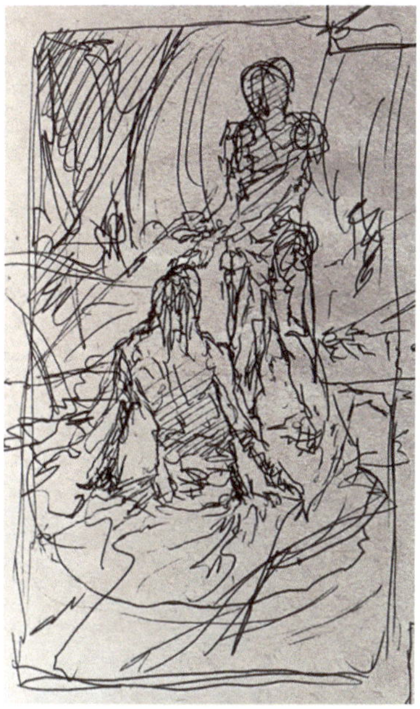

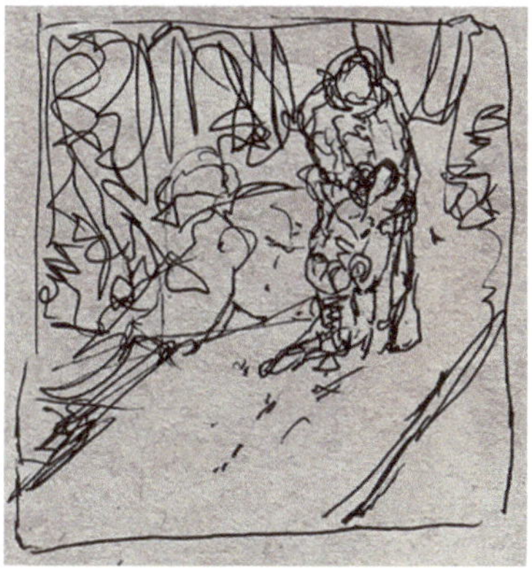

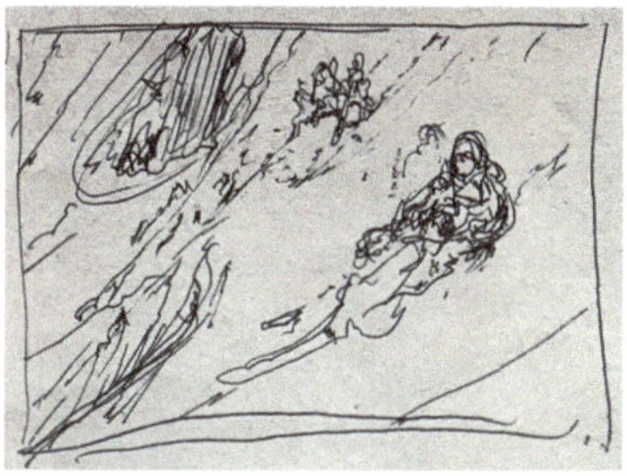

② **Rough Sketch**

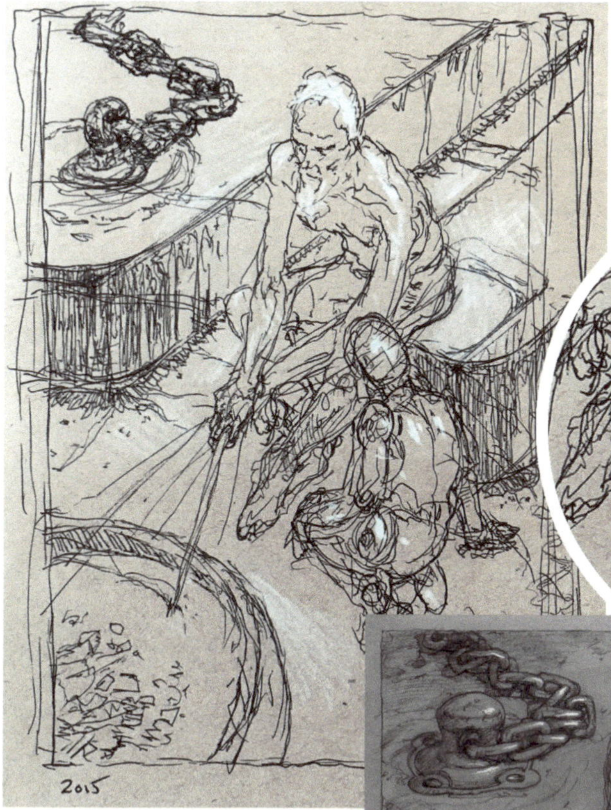

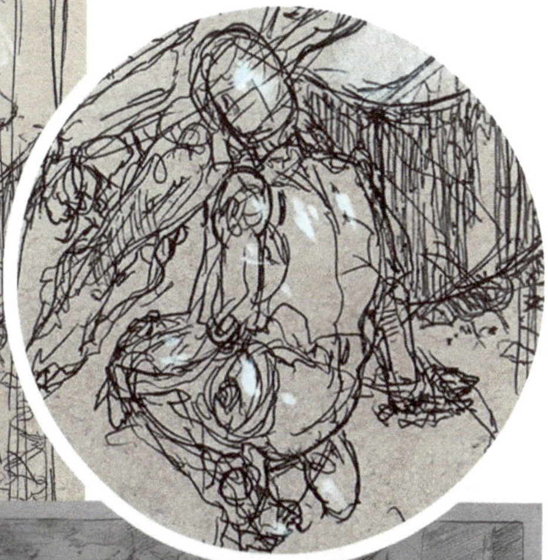

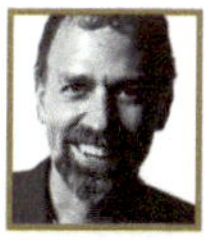

③ **Final Sketch**

Donato GIANCOLA

- www.donatoart.com
- donato@donatoart.com
- Prometheus
- Oil on panel 42"x 32"

Portrait photo by: Greg Preston

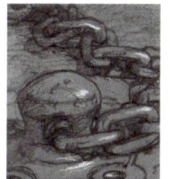
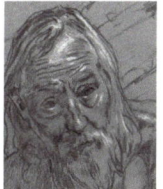
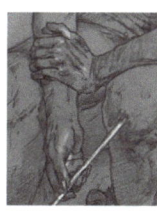
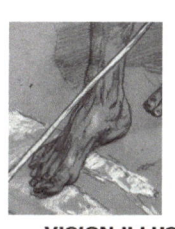
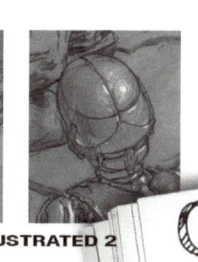
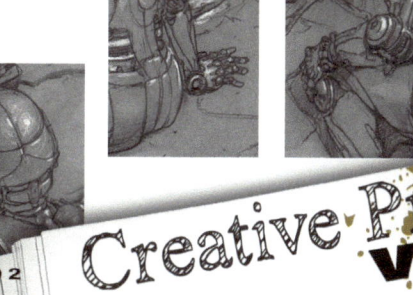
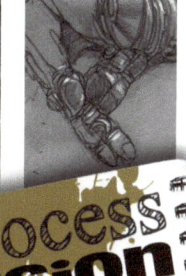

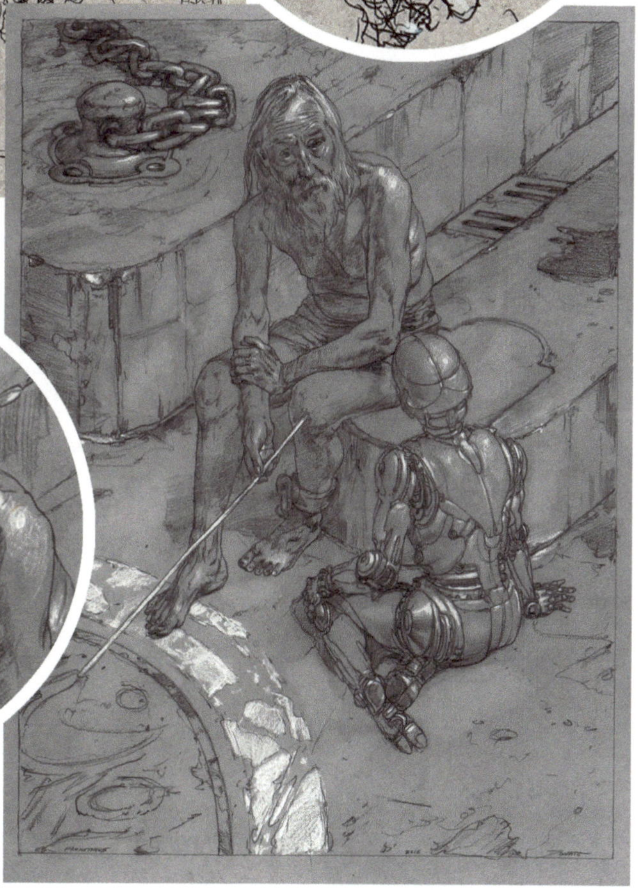

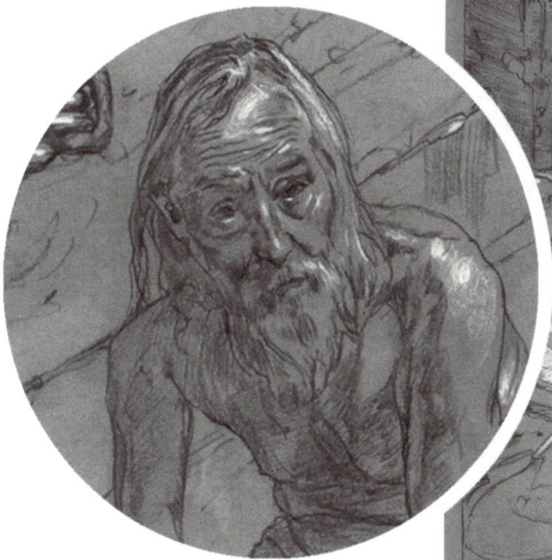

Creative Process — Vision Illustrated

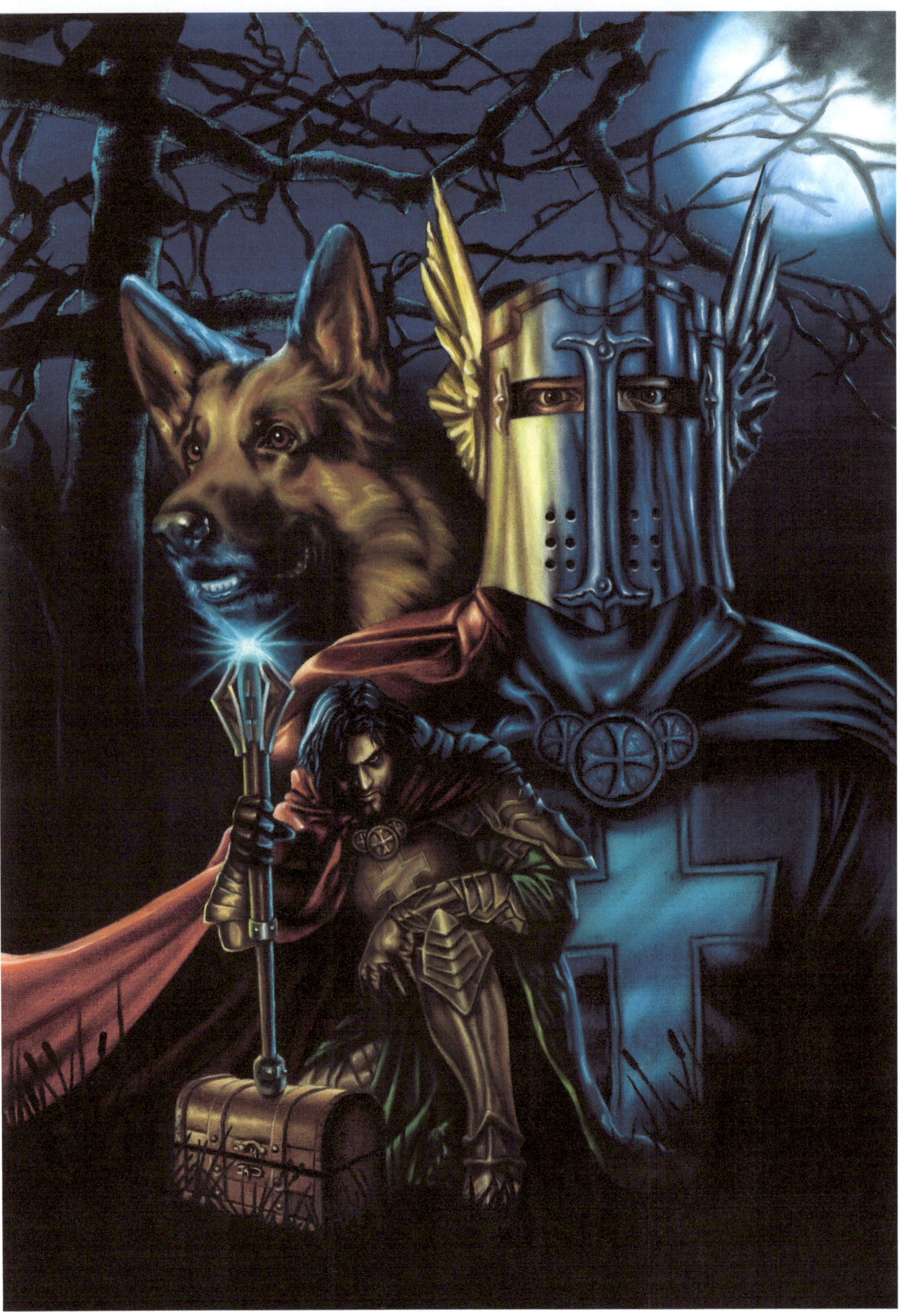

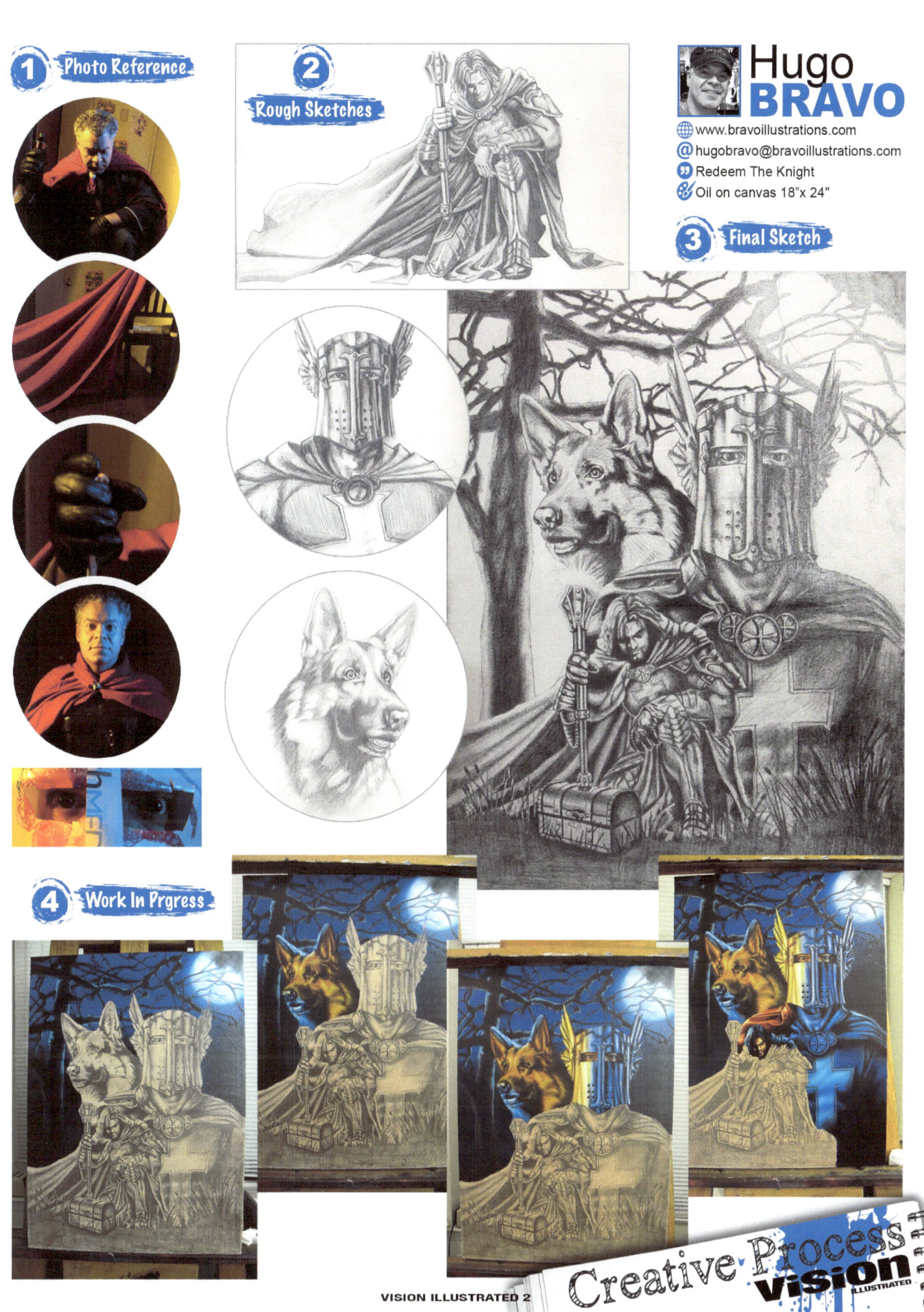

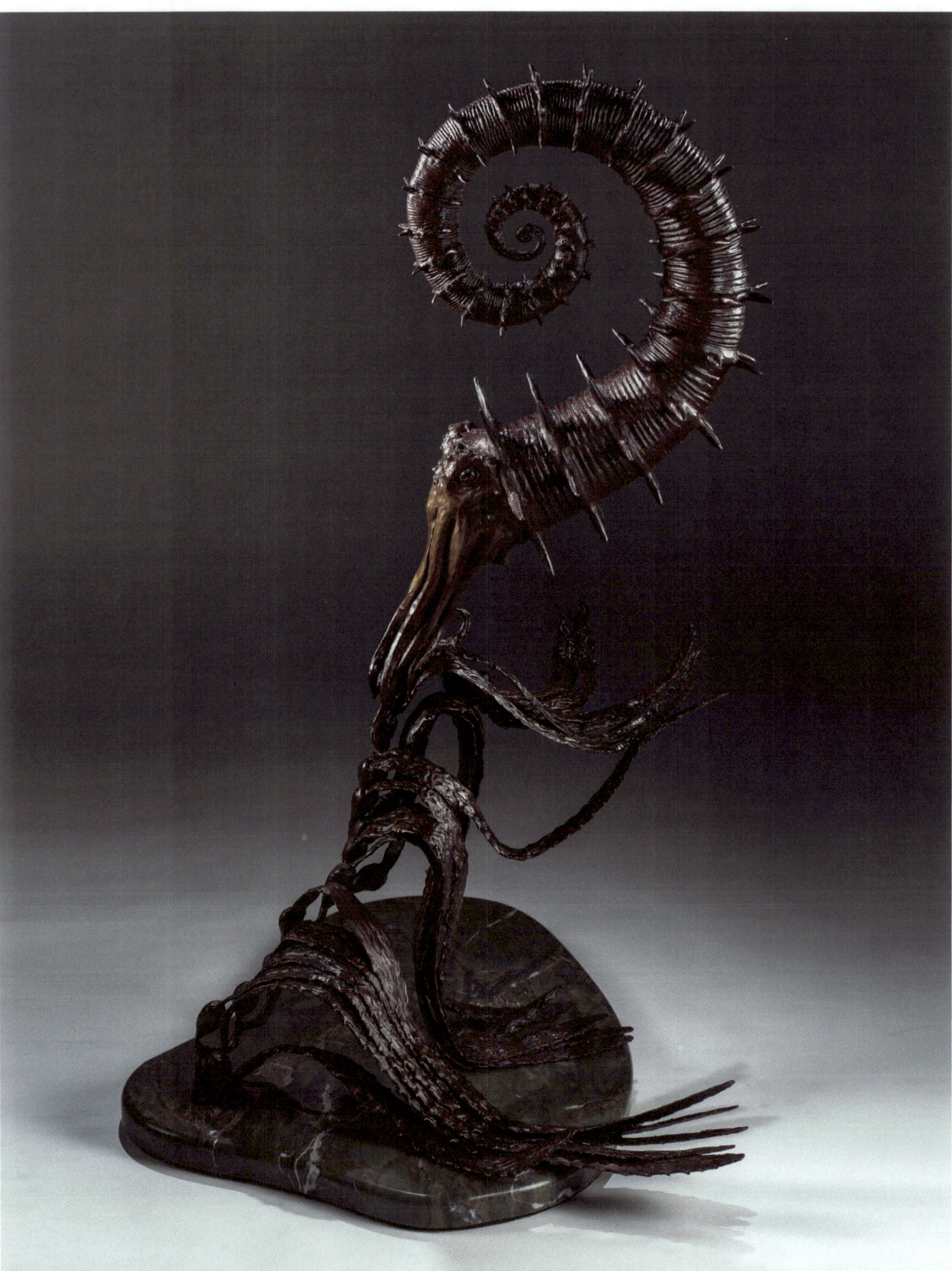

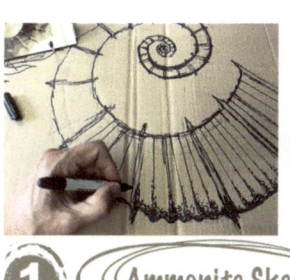 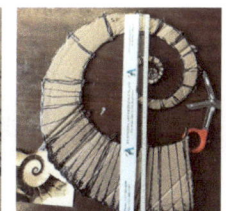 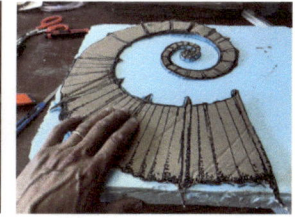 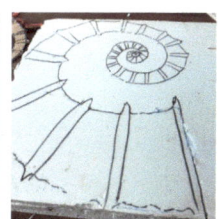

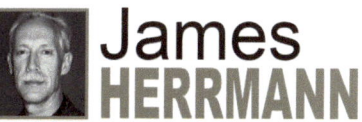

James HERRMANN

🌐 www.herrmannstudio.com
@ jmherrmann@fuse.net
📞 513-604-3096
💬 Heteromorph Ammonite
✂ 37"H x 27"W x 22"D

NSP Hard Sulfur Free Plasteline by Chavant over a foam and metal internal armature, Kelp leaves sculpted with Clayette Medium also by Chavant

1. Ammonite Sketch

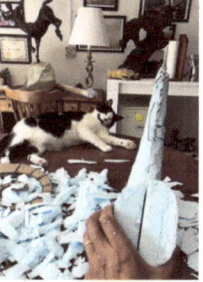 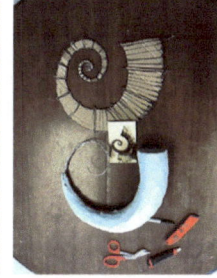 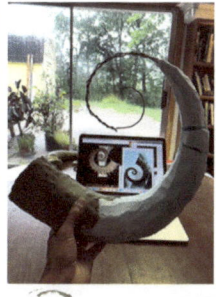 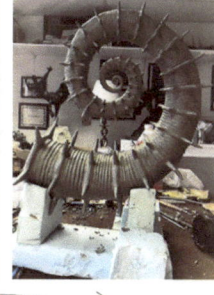

2. Foam Carving **3. Clay Overlay**

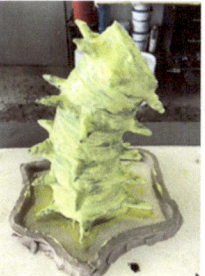 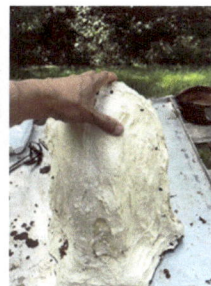 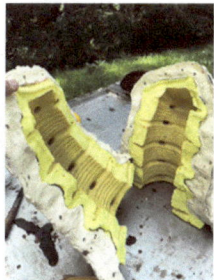 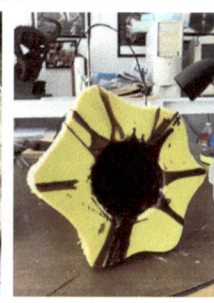

4. Mold

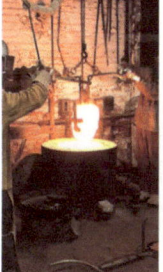 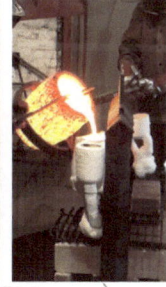 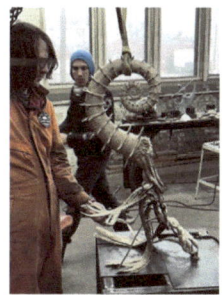 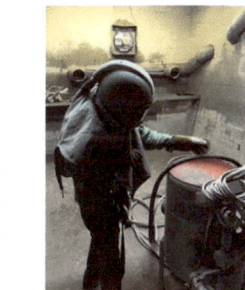

5. Molten Bronze **6. Bronze Welding** **7. Bronze Sand Blasting**

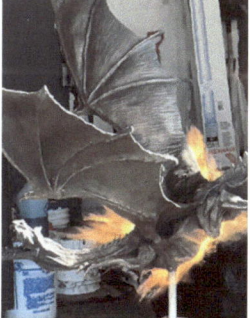 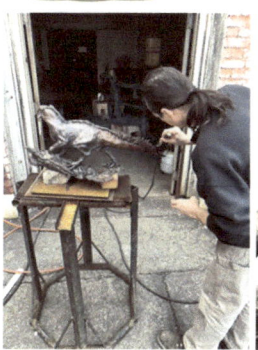

8. "Bolt from the Blue" being heated to apply the ferric nitrate

9. "Aquilops Americanus" with wax being brushed

Creative Process — Vision Illustrated

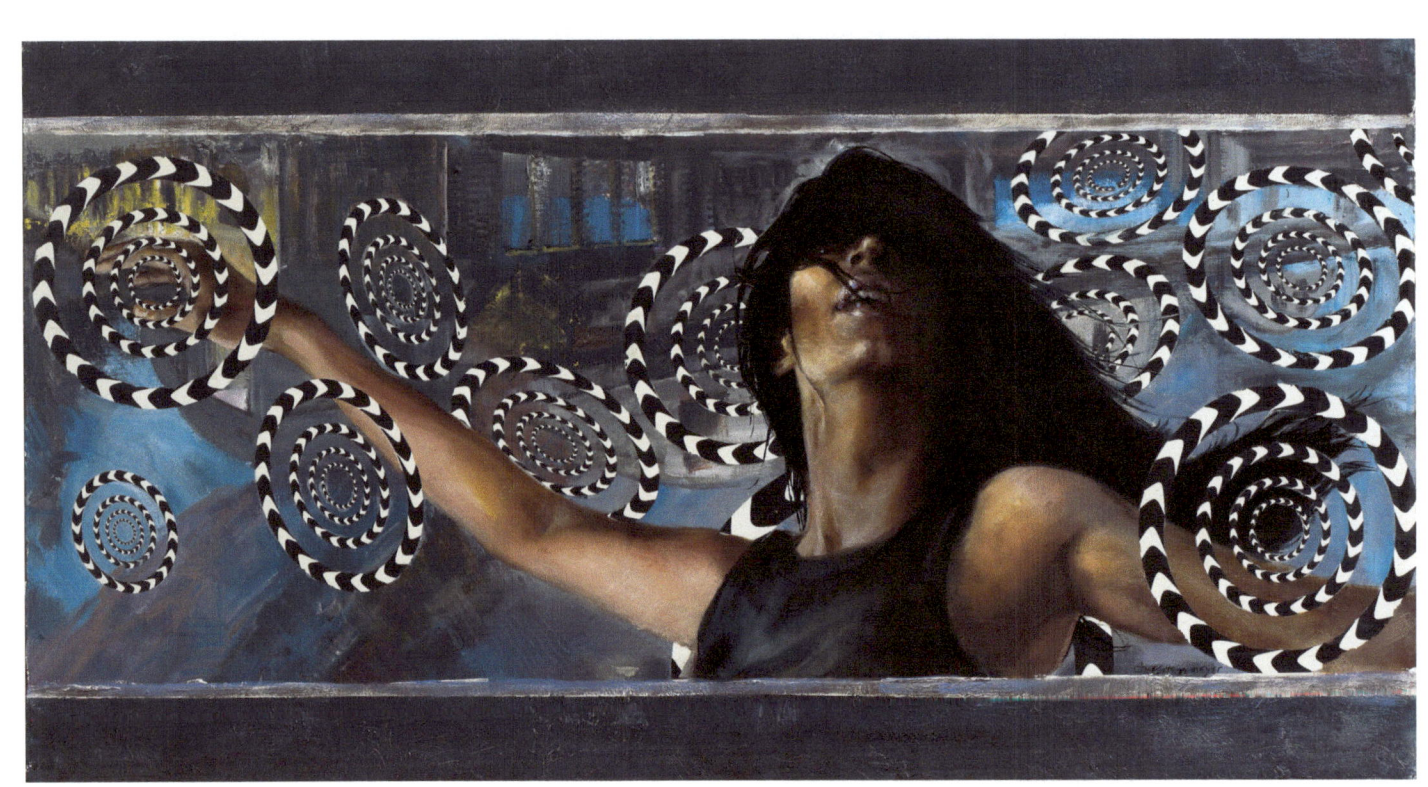

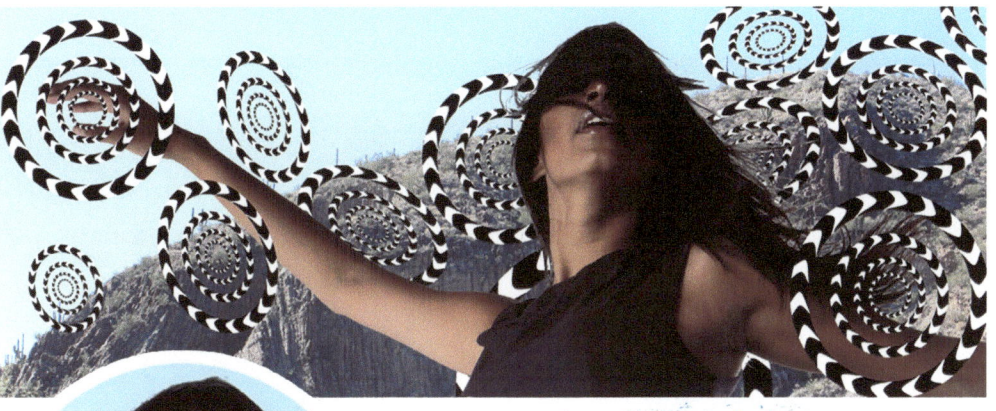

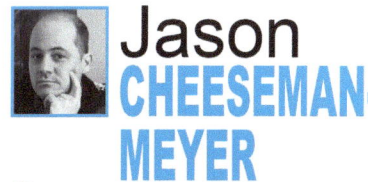

Jason CHEESEMAN-MEYER

- www.cheeseman-meyer.com
- jasoncmeyer.com
- @ jasoncmeyer@gmail.com
- Discobolus
- Oil on paper mounted to panel 11"x24"

1 Photo Reference

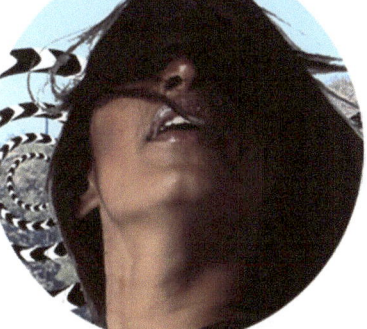

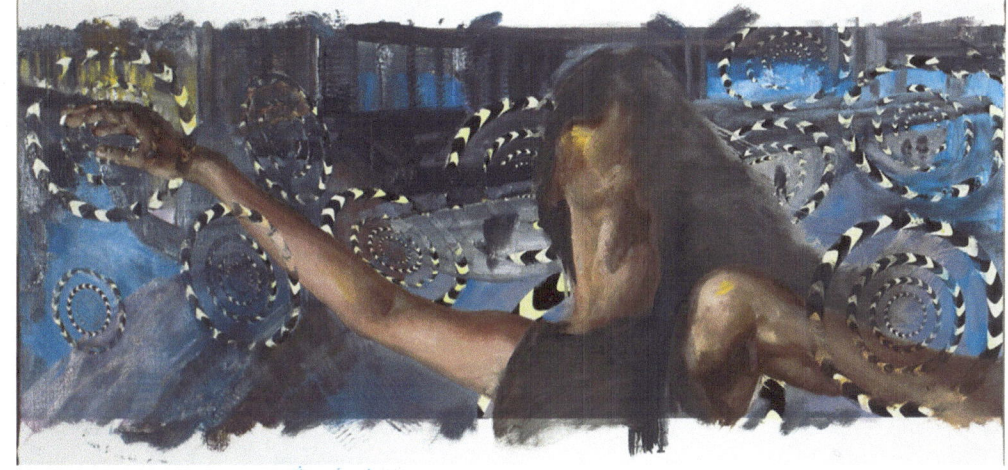

2 Underpainting

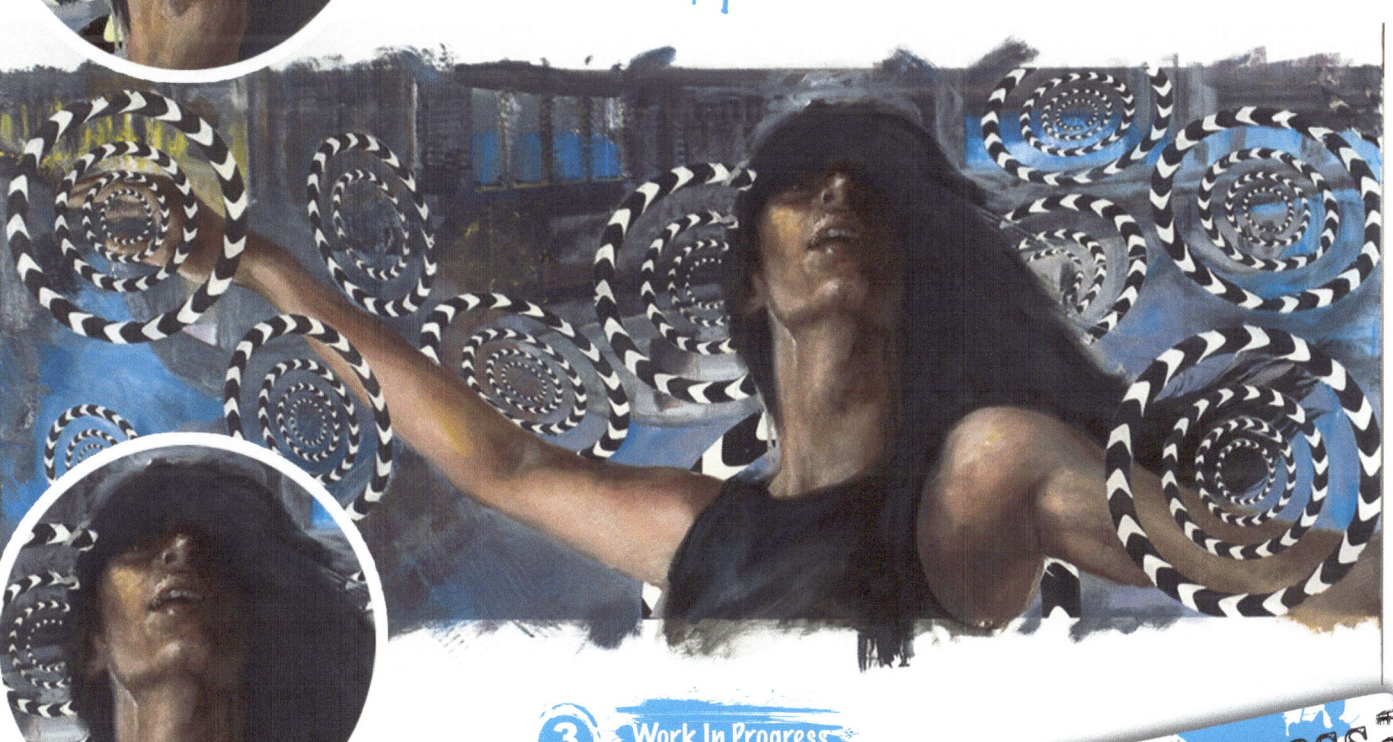

3 Work In Progress

VISION ILLUSTRATED 2

Creative Process

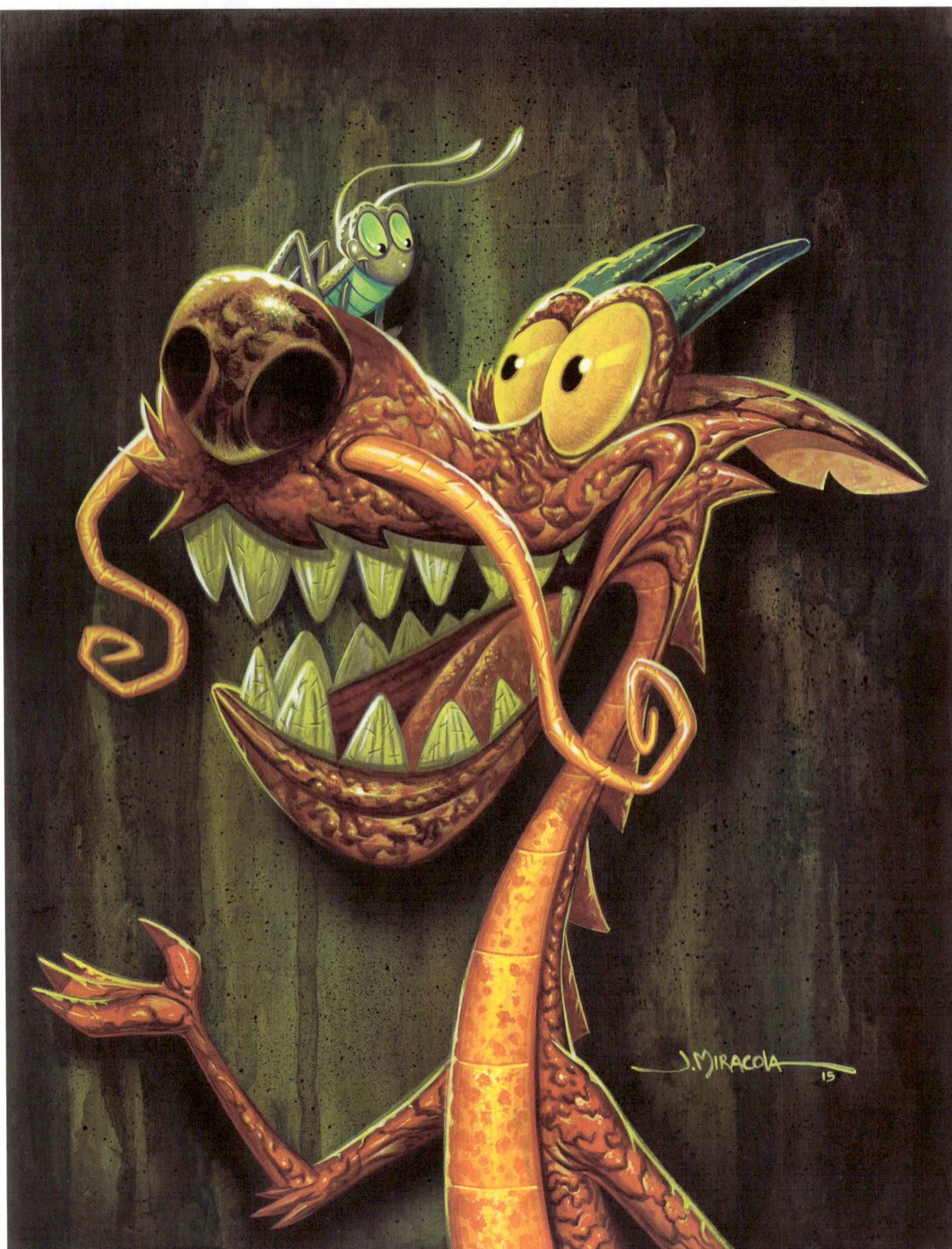

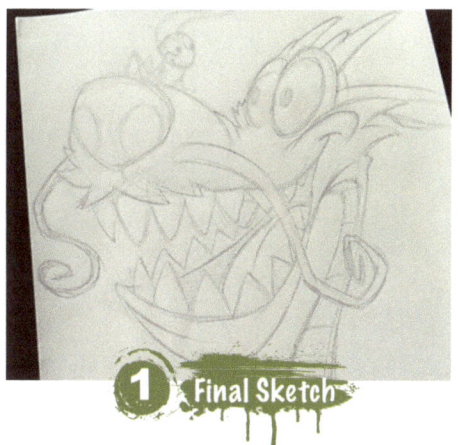
1. Final Sketch

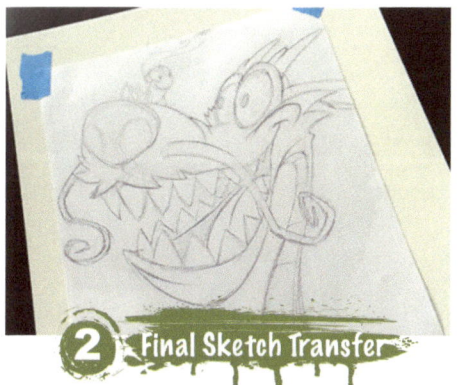
2. Final Sketch Transfer

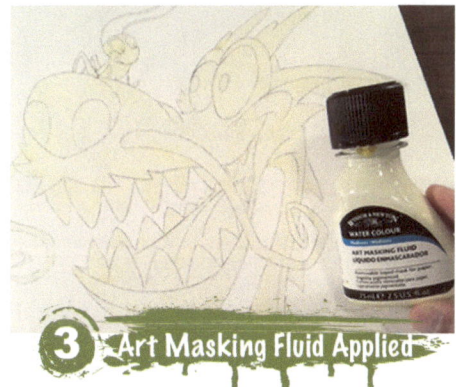
3. Art Masking Fluid Applied

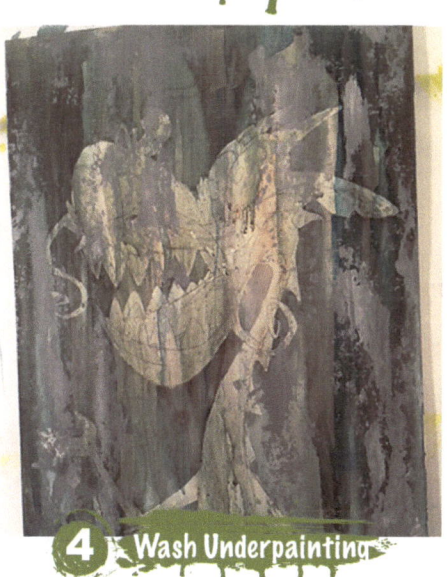
4. Wash Underpainting

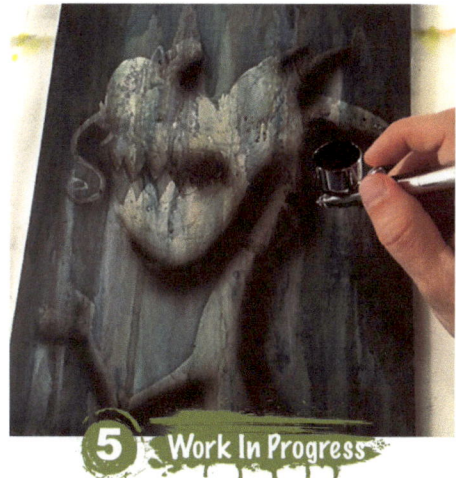
5. Work In Progress

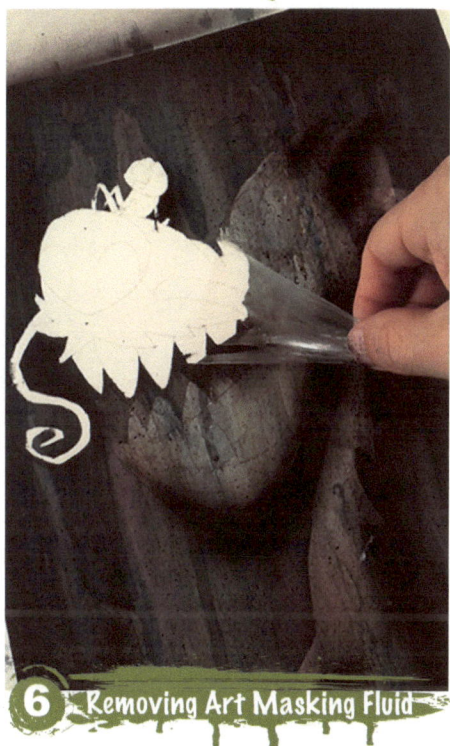
6. Removing Art Masking Fluid

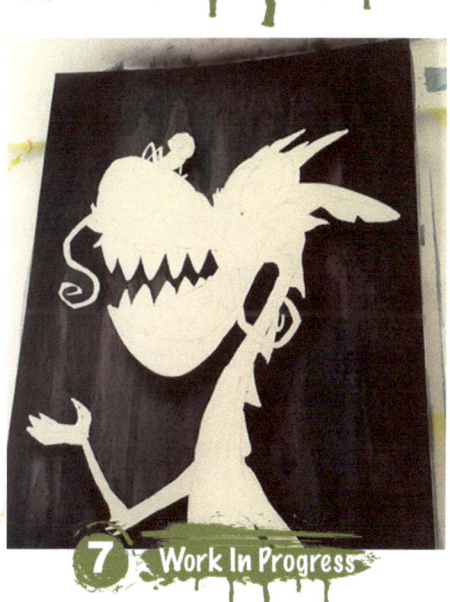
7. Work In Progress

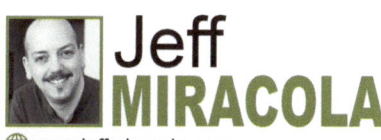

Jeff MIRACOLA

www.jeffmiracola.com
Mushu and Crickee
Acrylic on illustration board 11"x14"

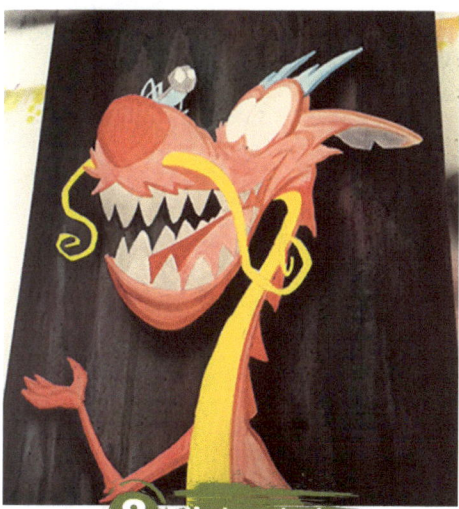
8. Underpainting

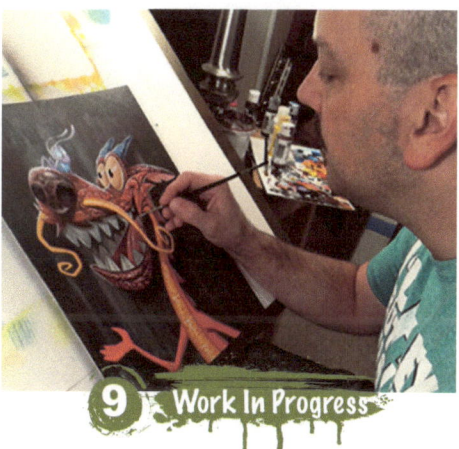
9. Work In Progress

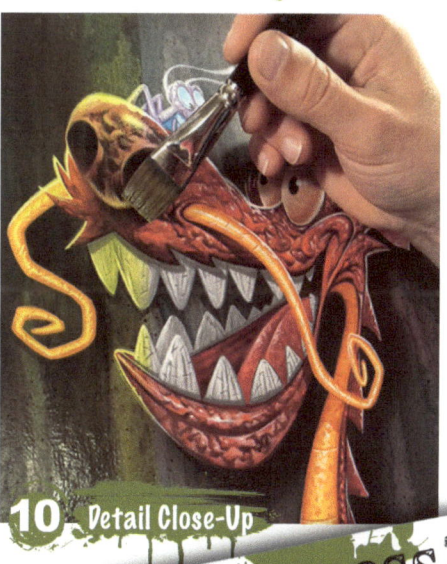
10. Detail Close-Up

Creative Process Vision ILLUSTRATED

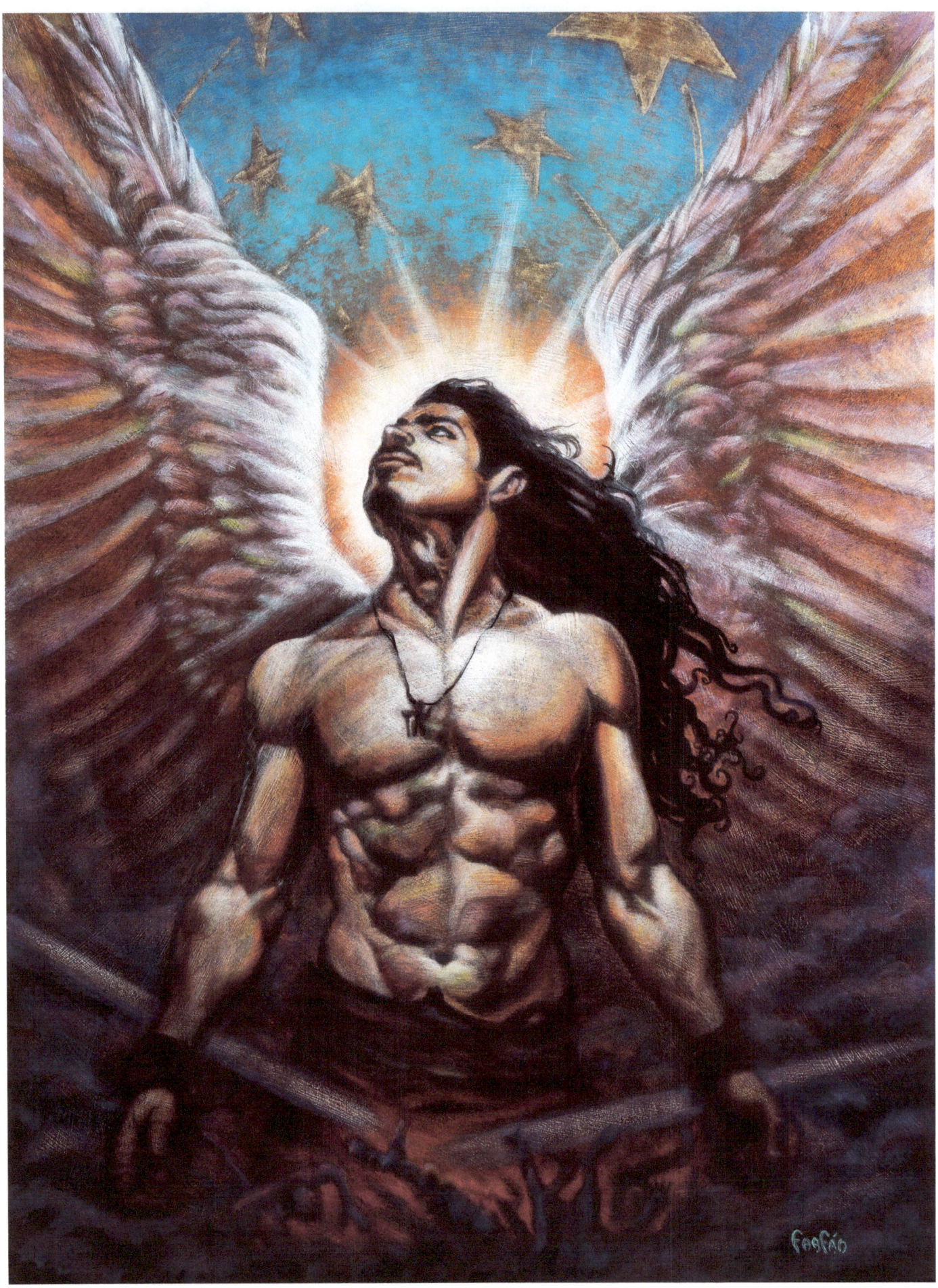

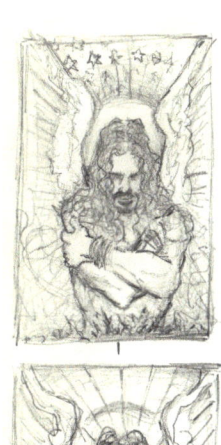
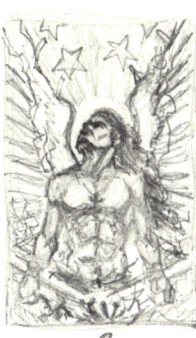
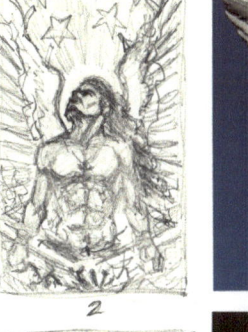
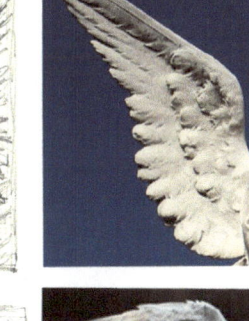
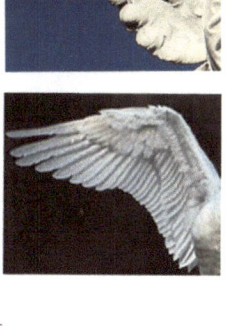

1 Thumbnails

2 Photo Reference
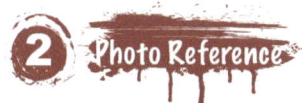
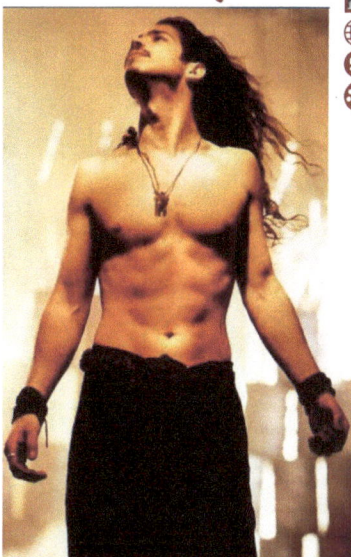

Jorge FARFÁN

www.jorgefarfanartist.com
Rebirth Ritual
Oil on cold press illustration board
18"x 24"
(Chris Cornell photo © Marty Temme)

3 Rough Sketch
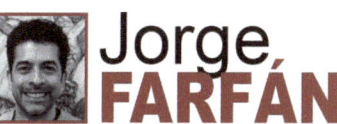
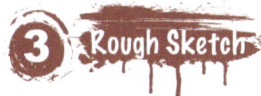
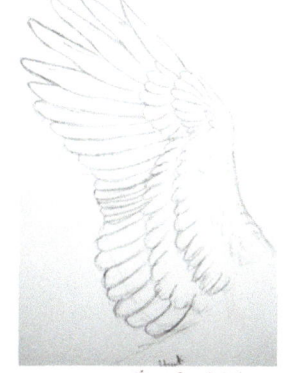

4 Final Sketch
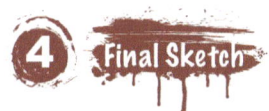
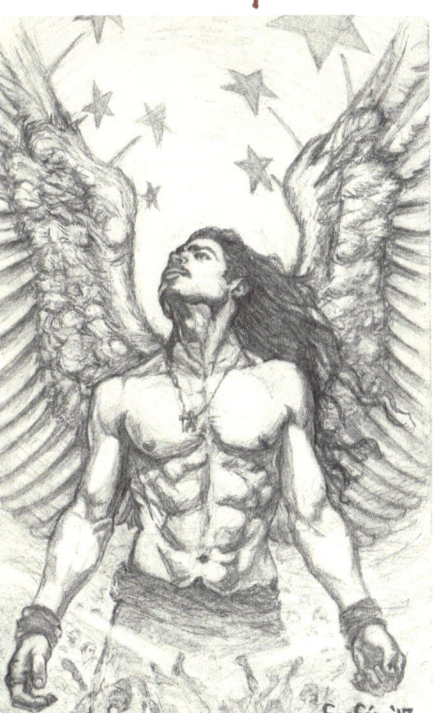

5 Color Rough
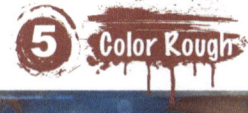
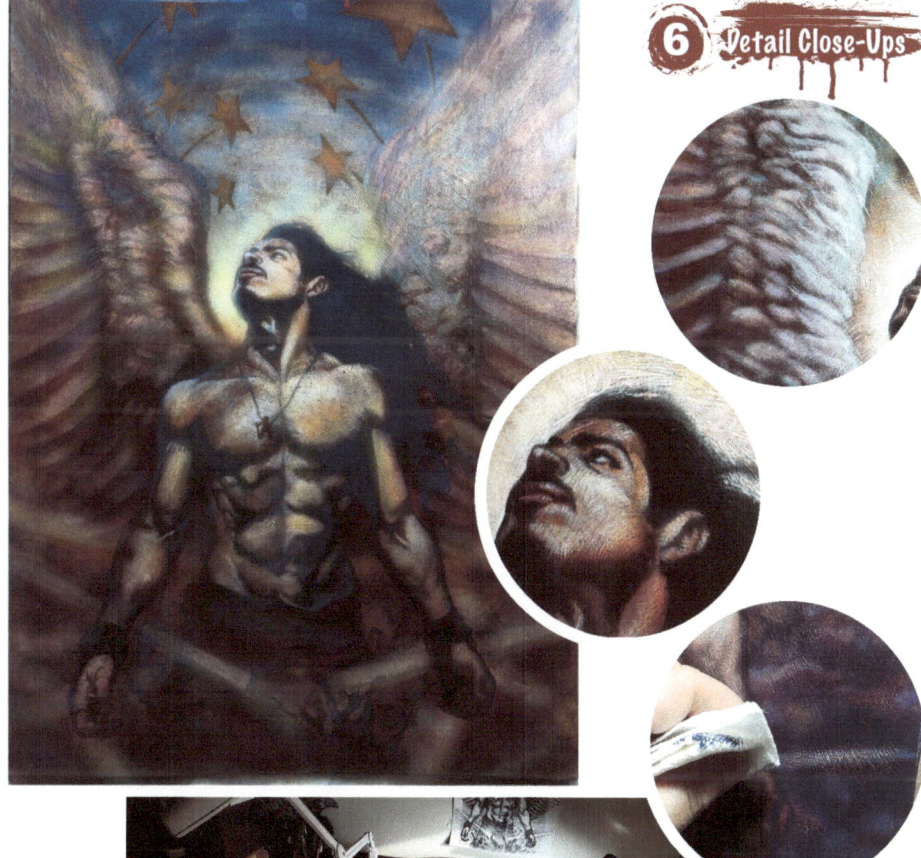

6 Detail Close-Ups

7 Work In Progress
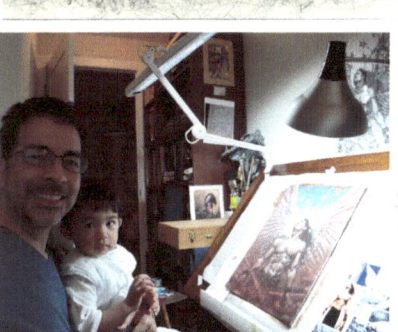
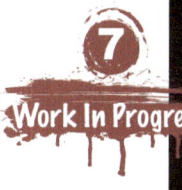

Creative Process

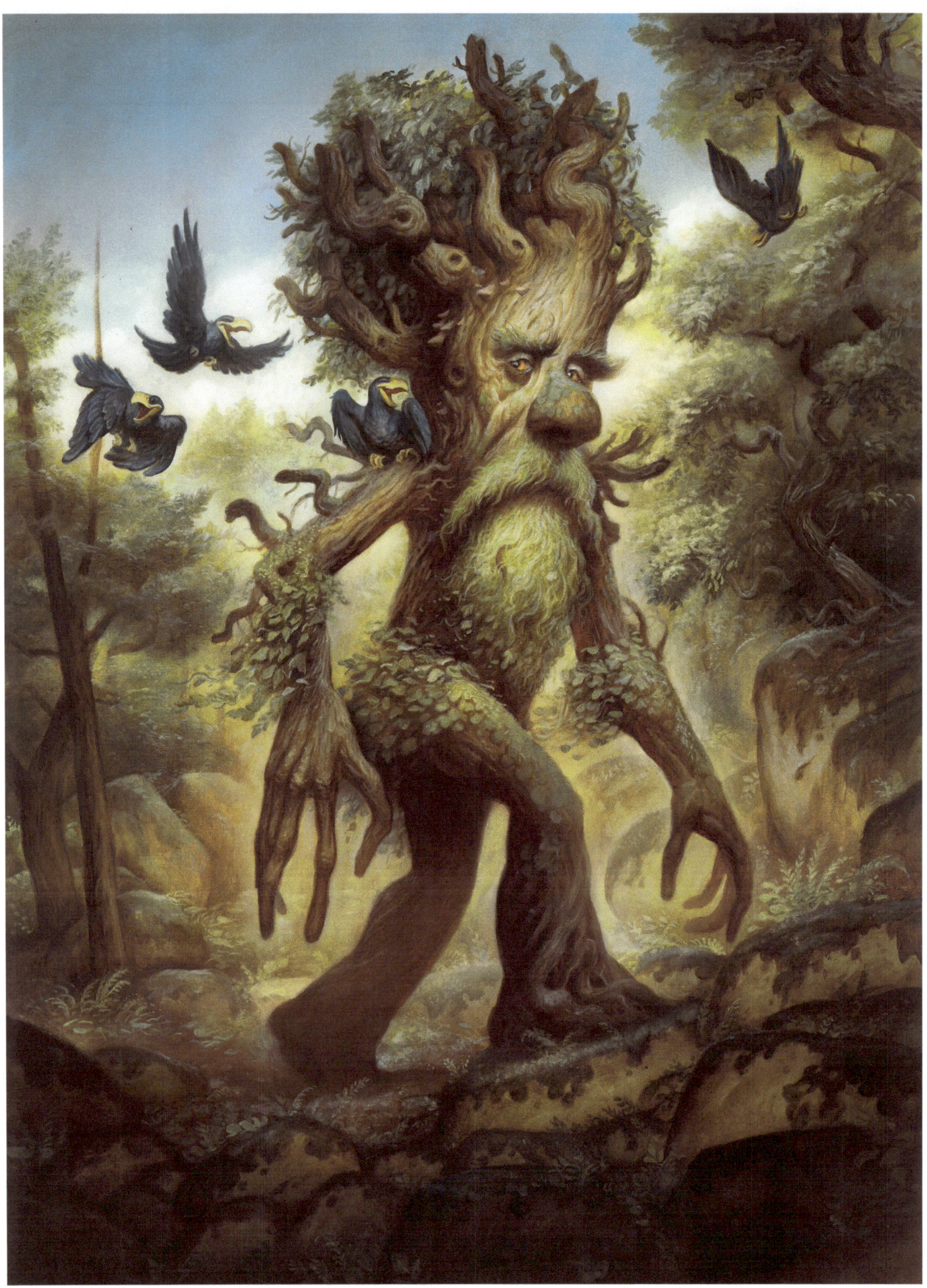

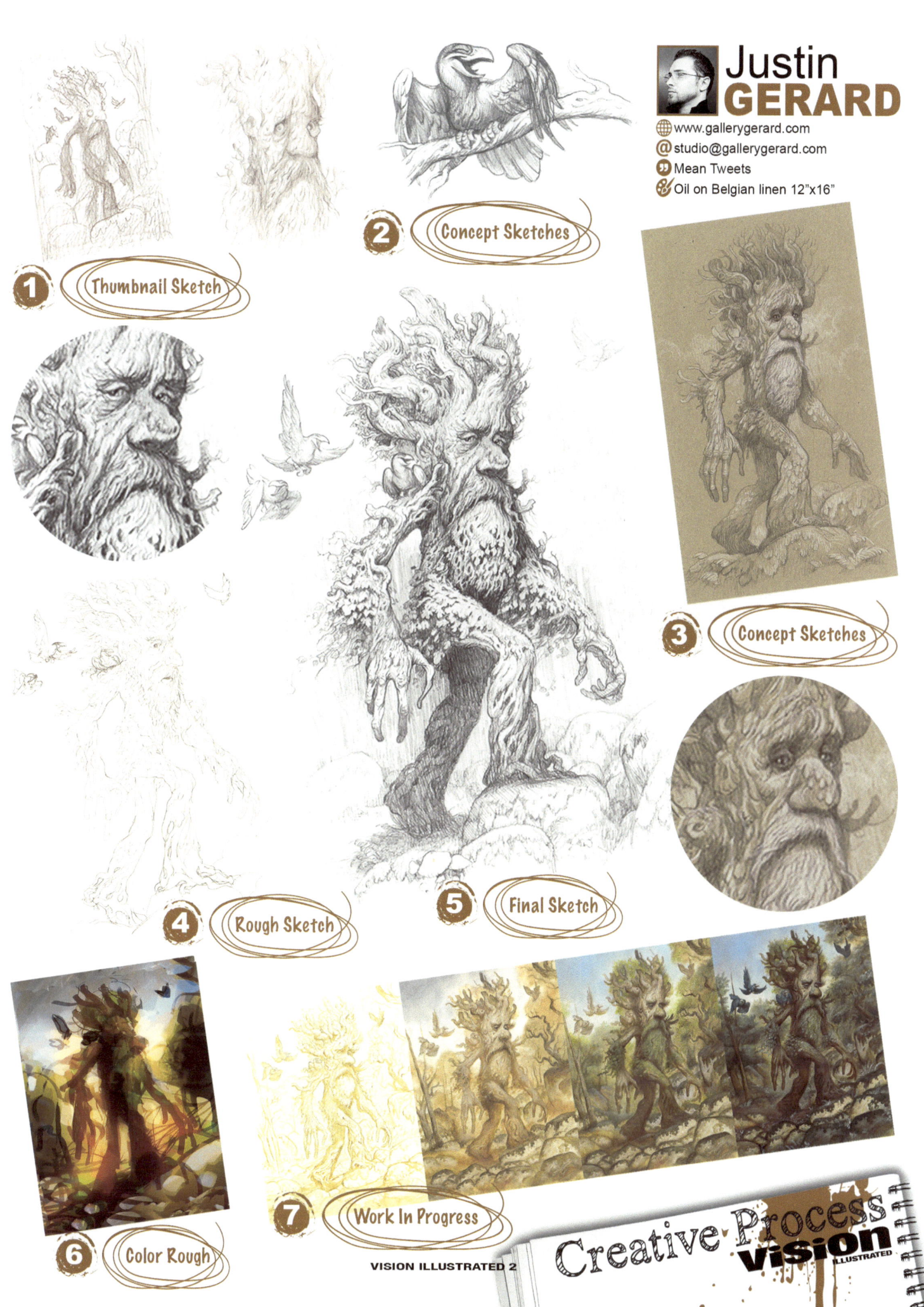

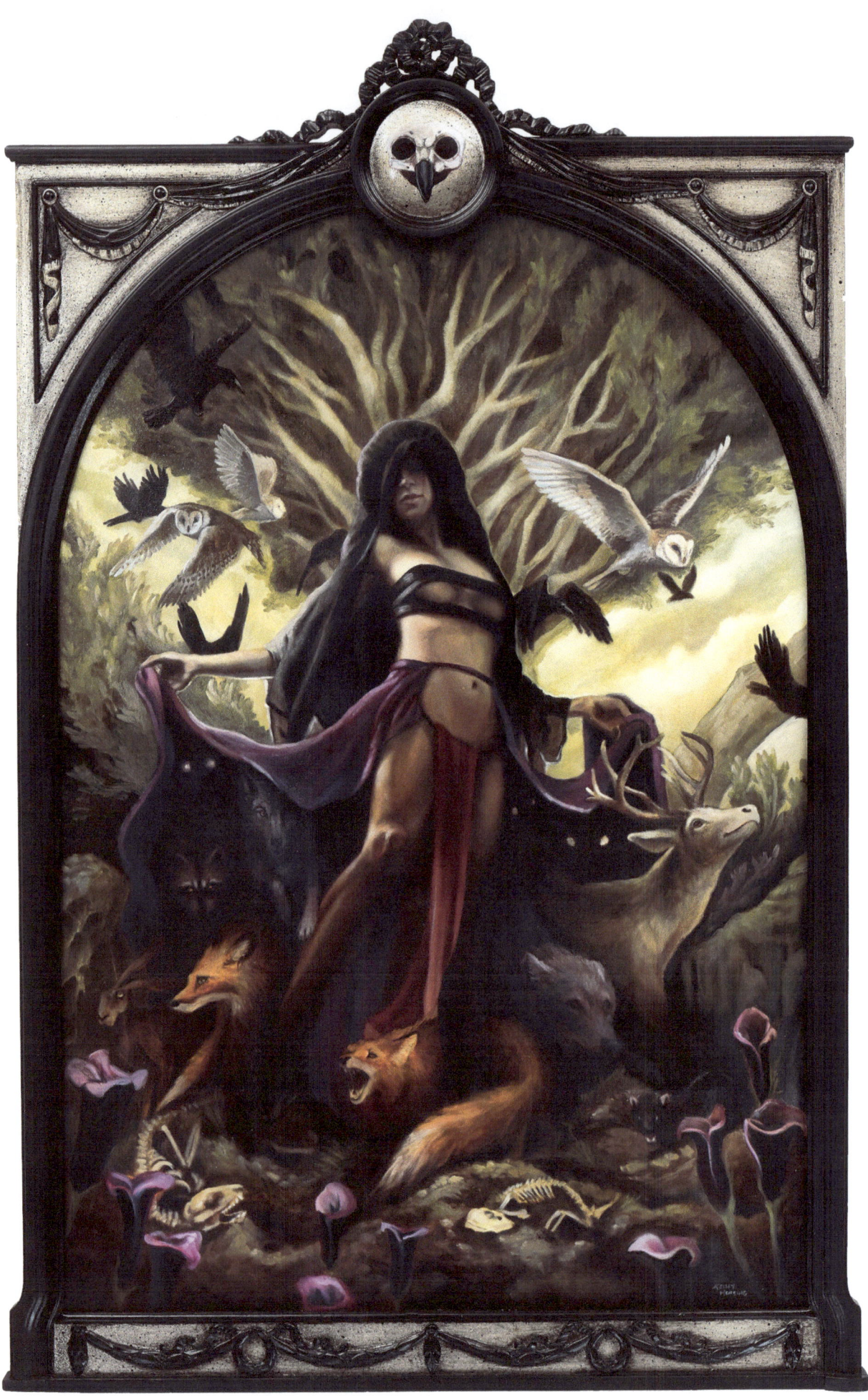

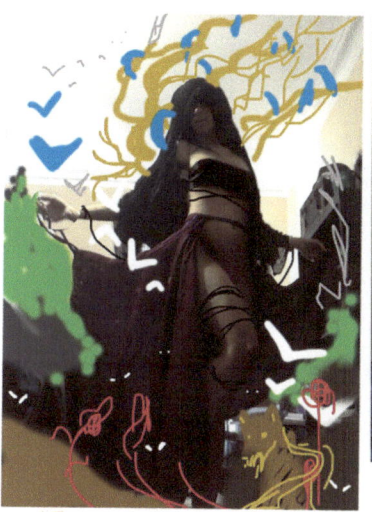
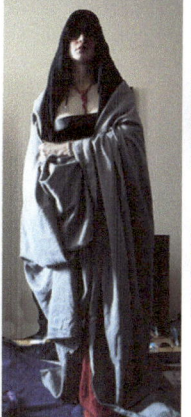
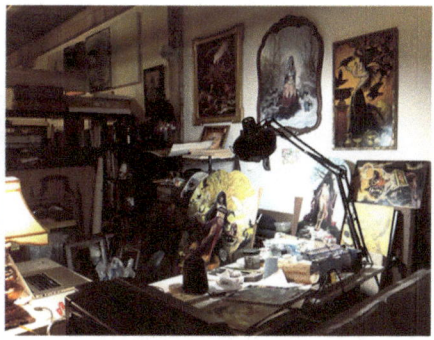

1 Photo Reference

2 The Studio

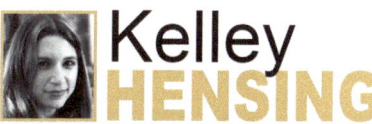

Kelley HENSING

🌐 www.kelleyhensing.com
@ kelleyhensing@gmail.com
🎵 Revenge of the Wild
🖌 Oil on wood panel 32"x48"
Re-finished antique frame

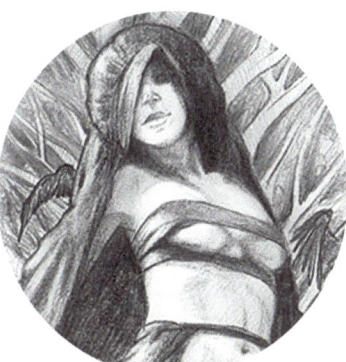

5 Detail Close-Up

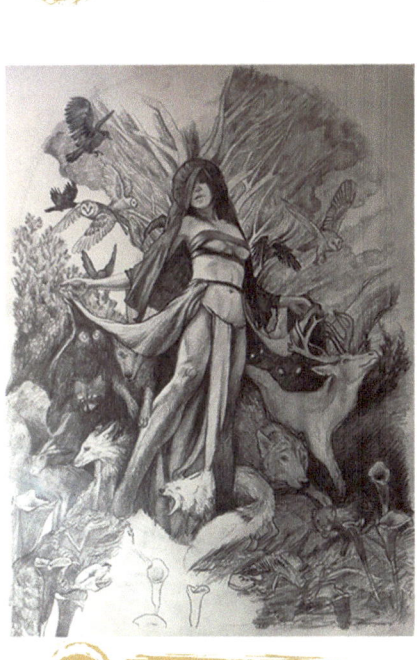

3 Sketch In Progress

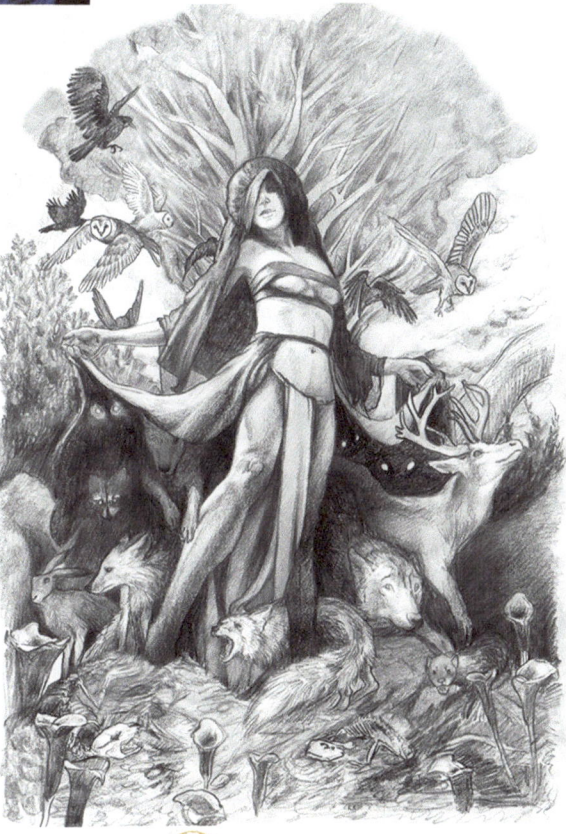

4 Final Sketch

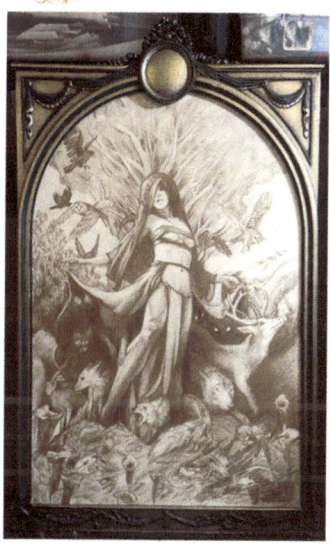

7 Testing Frame

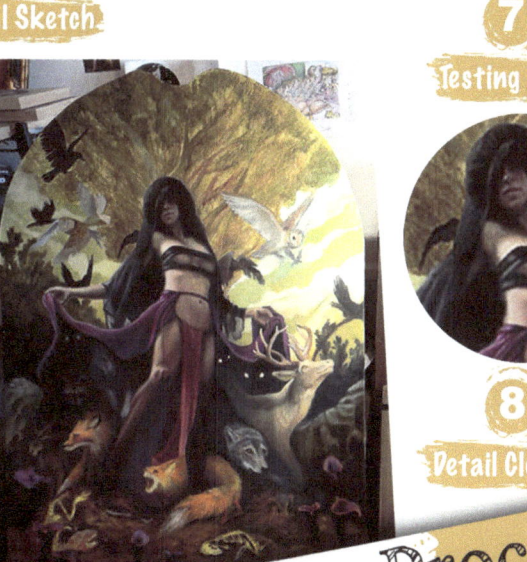

8 Detail Close-Up

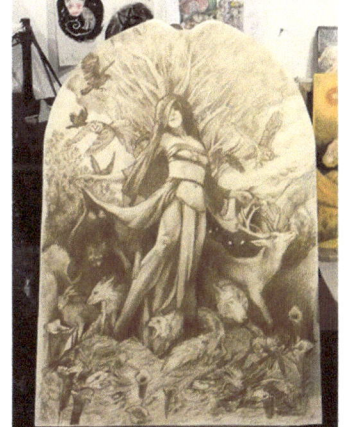

6 Work In Progress

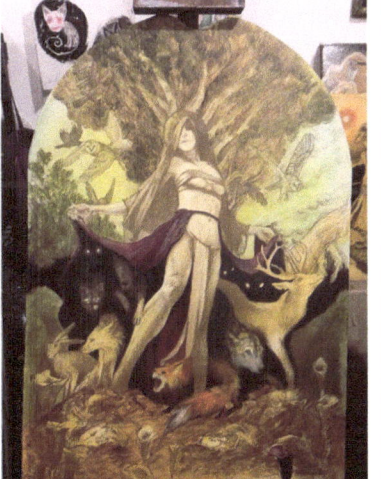

Creative Process — Vision Illustrated

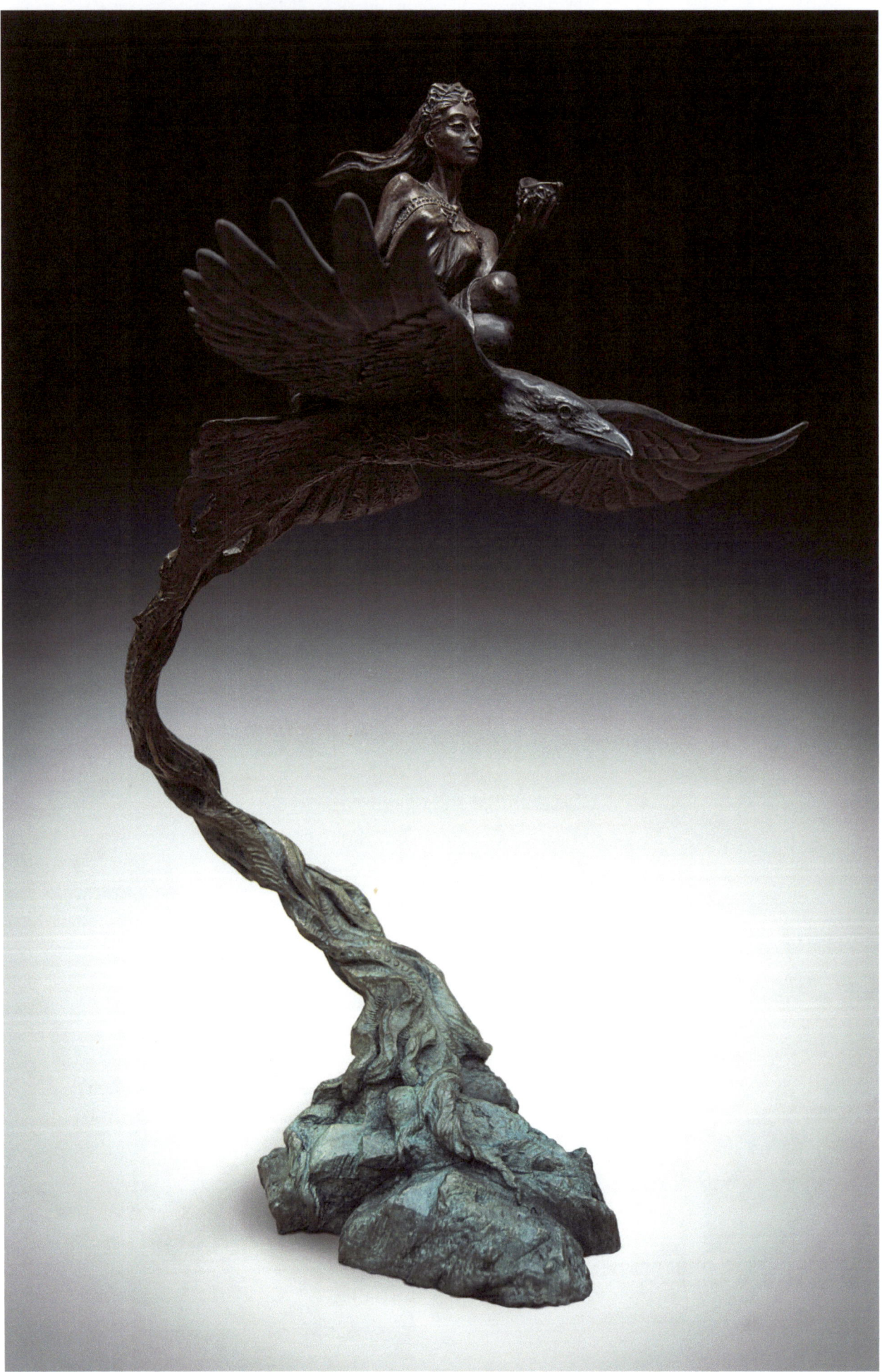

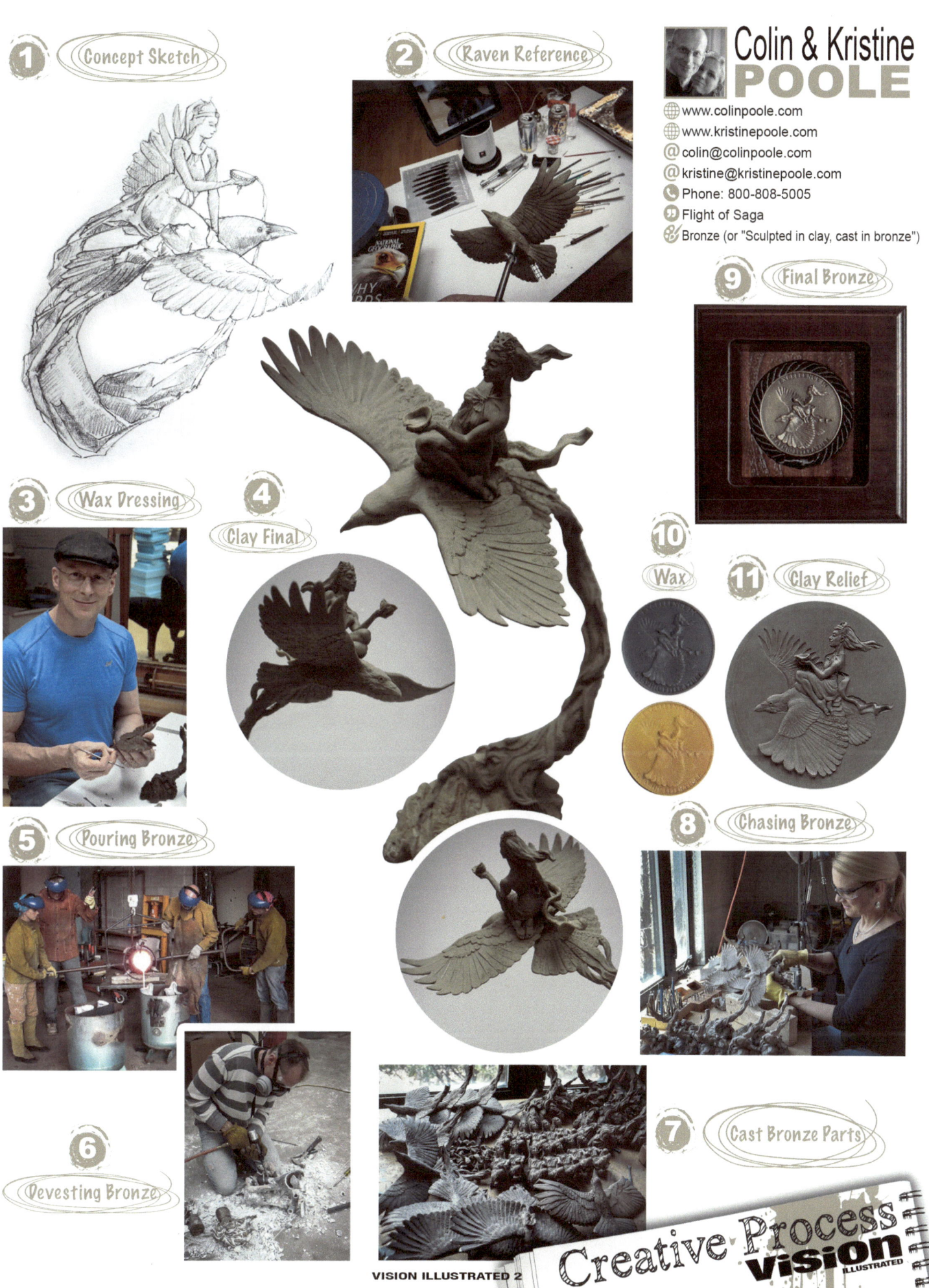

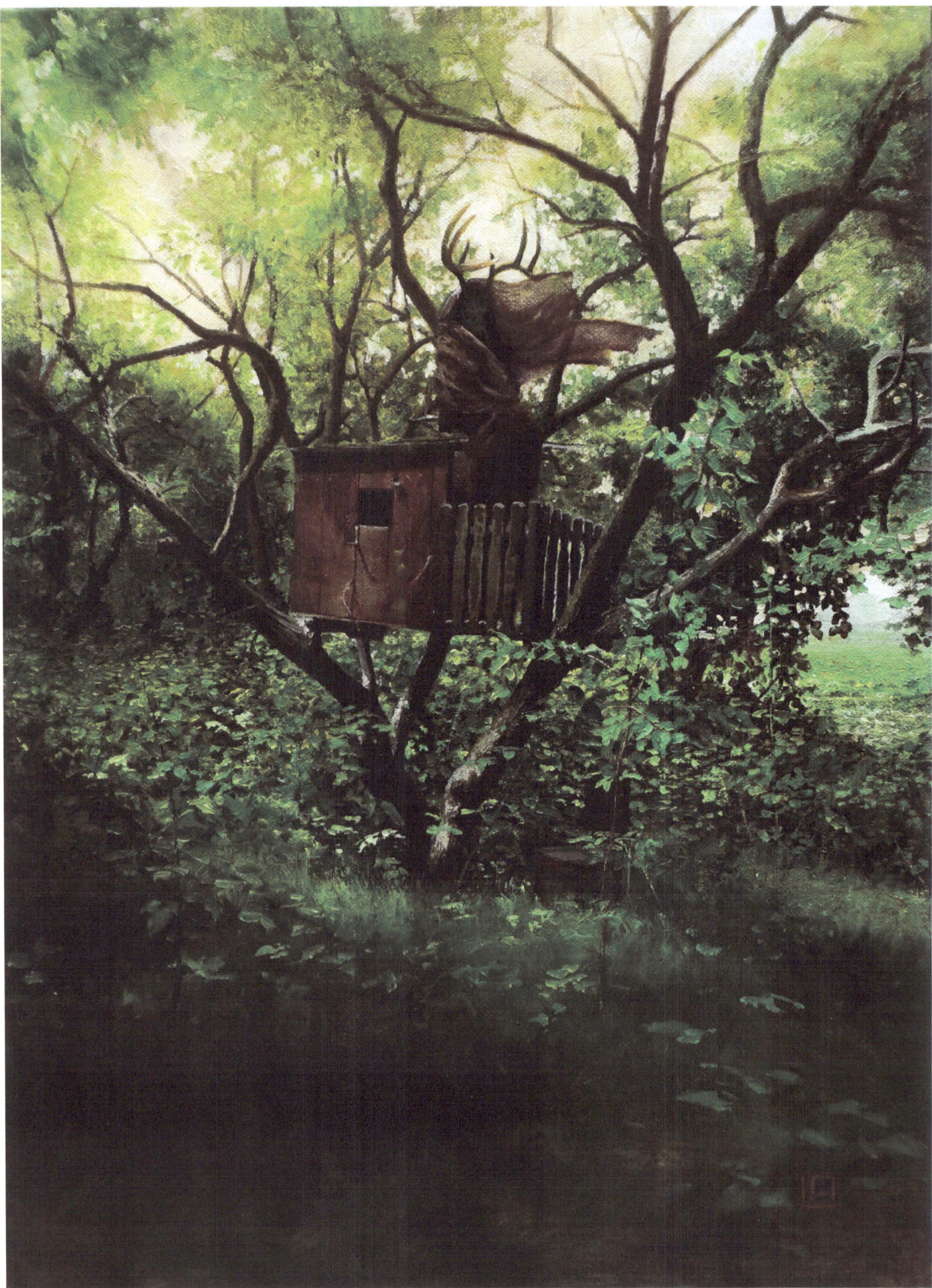

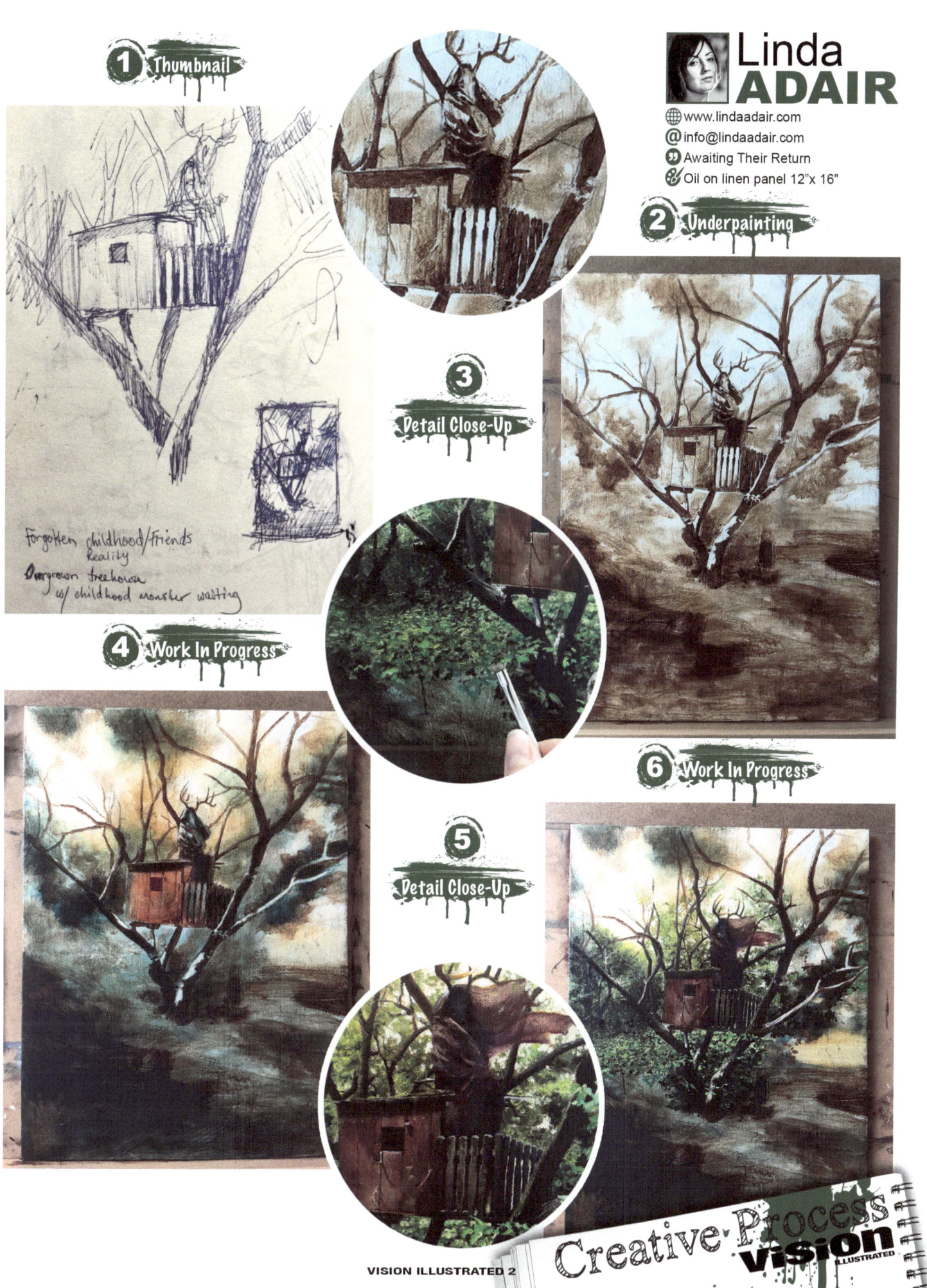

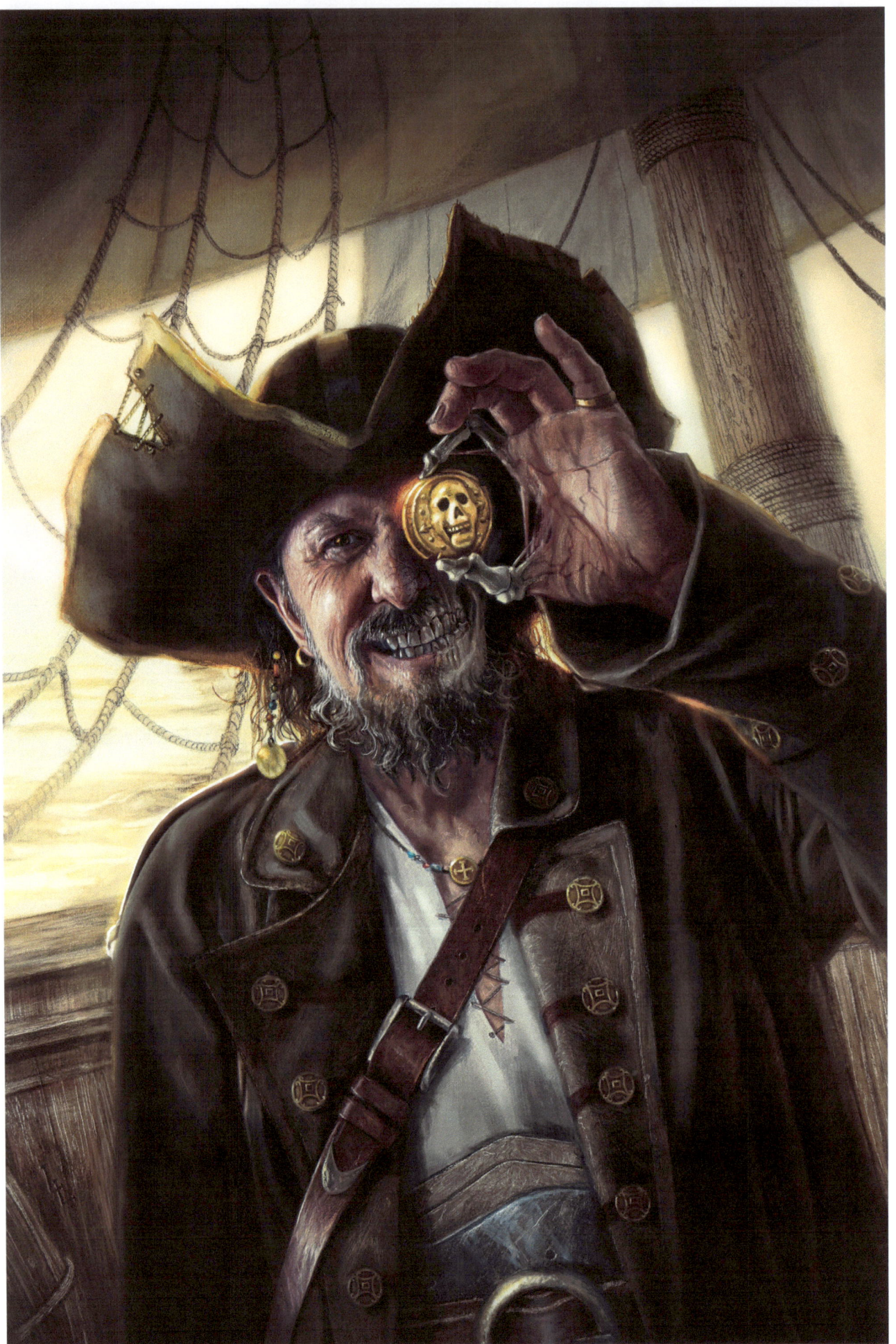

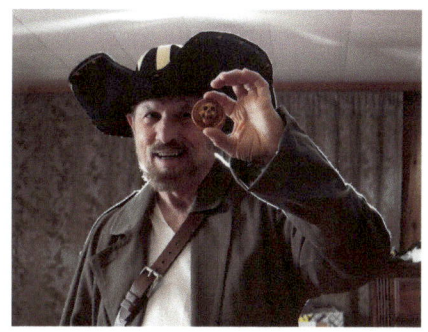

1 Photo Reference

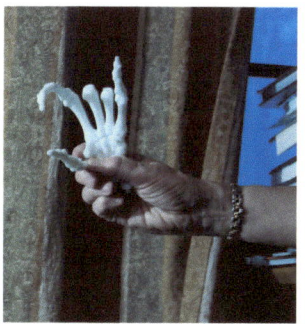

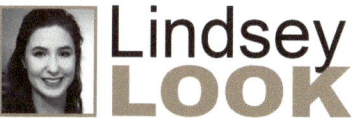
Lindsey LOOK
www.lindseylook.com
@ LindseyLook@gmail.com
" Dread Curse Captain
🎨 Oil on illustration board 13"x 19"

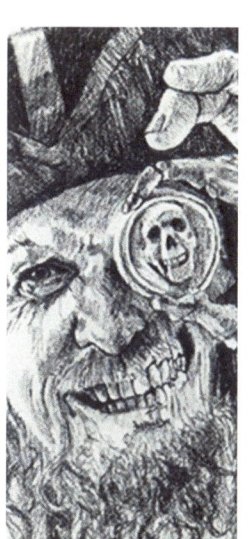
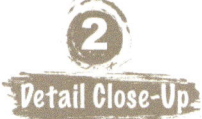
2 Detail Close-Up

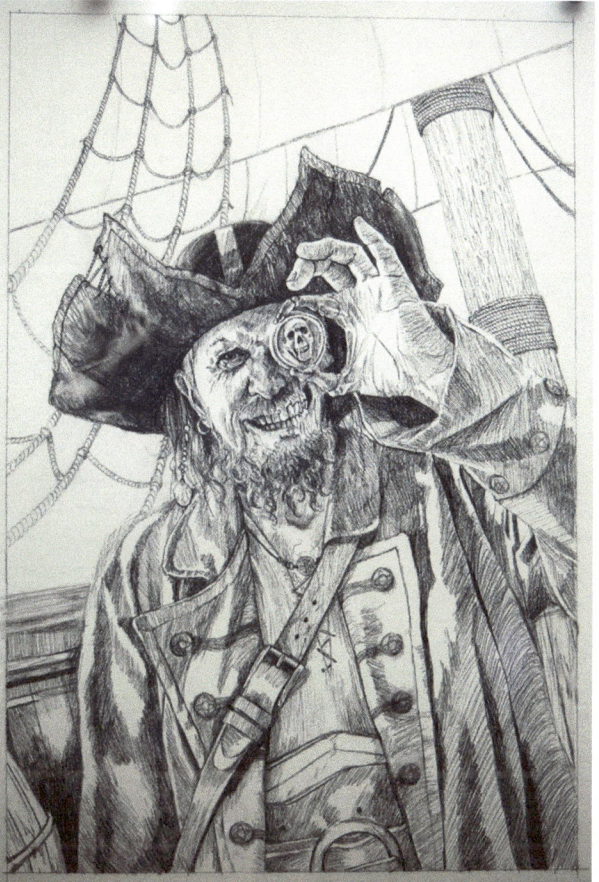
3 Final Sketch

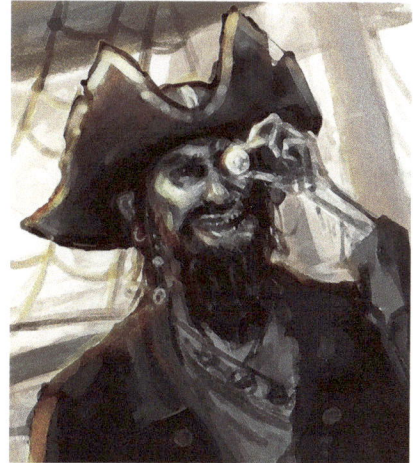
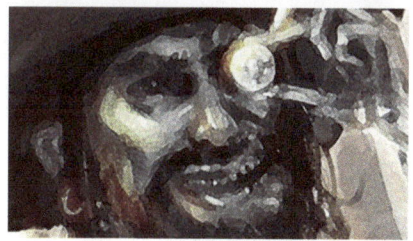
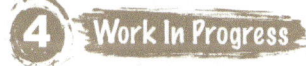
4 Work In Progress

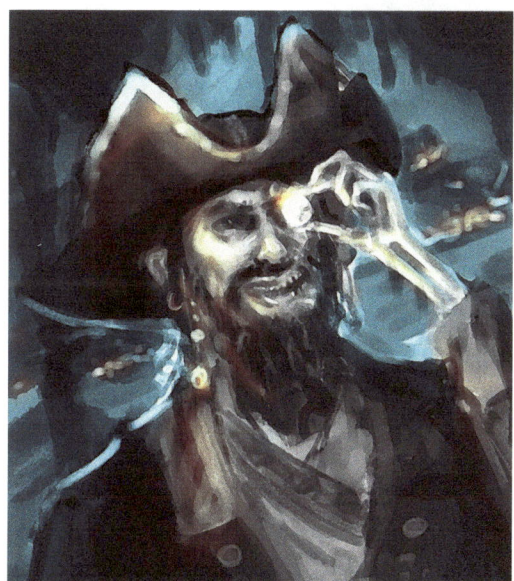
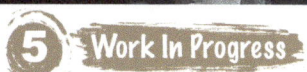
5 Work In Progress

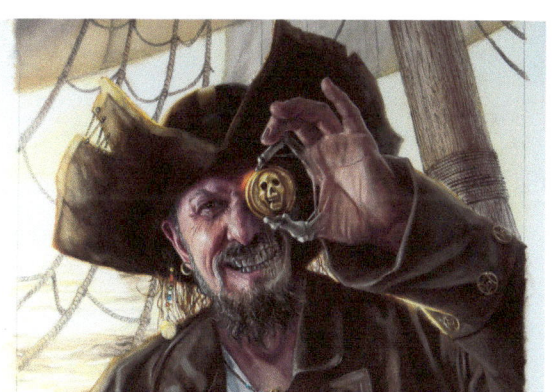
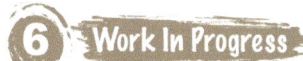
6 Work In Progress

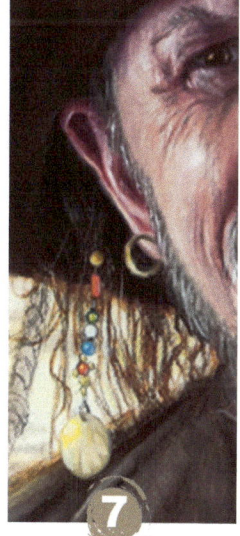
7 Detail Close-Up

Creative Process
VISION ILLUSTRATED 2

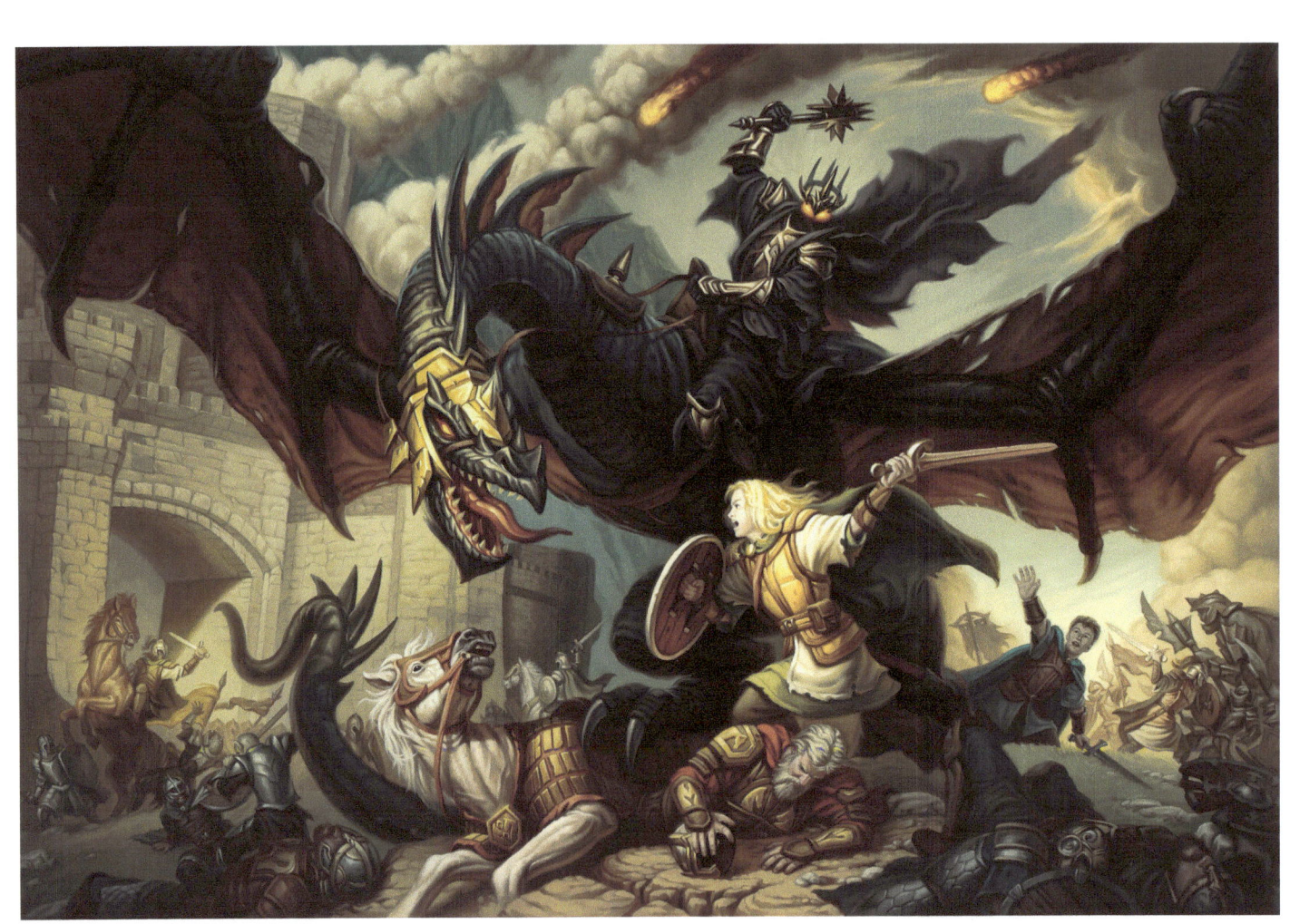

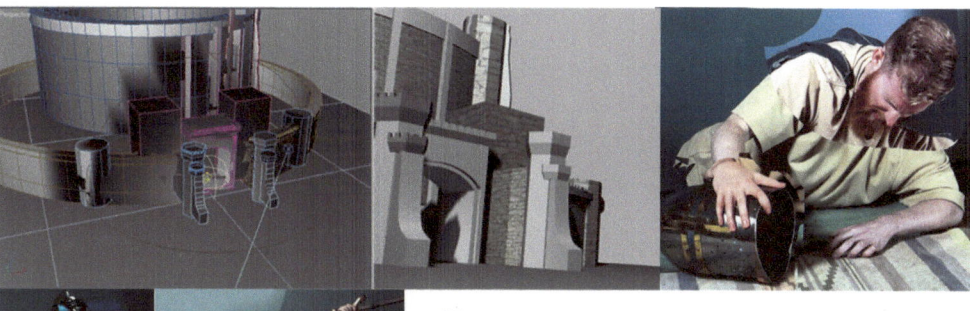
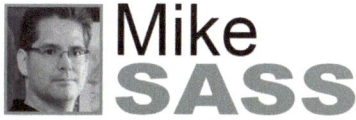

Mike SASS

www.sassart.com
mike@sassart.com
Éowyn and the Witch-King of Angmar
Oil on panel 36"x 24"

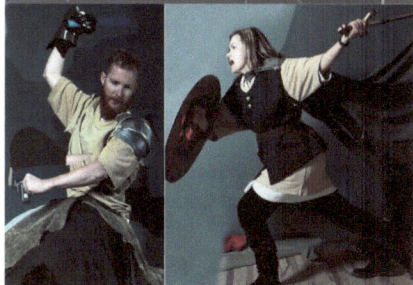

1 Photo Reference

2 Final Drawing

3 Underpaintings

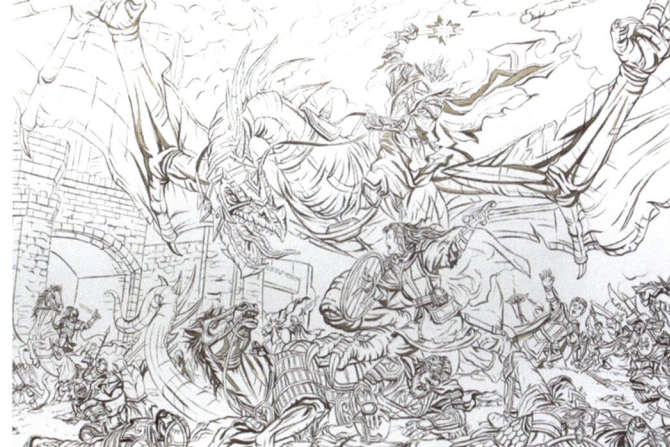

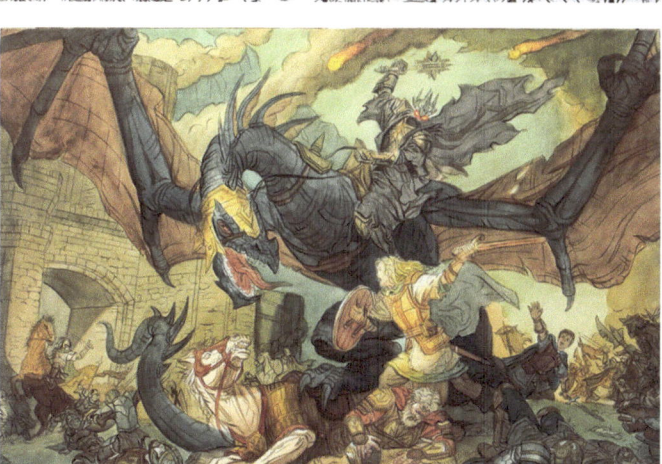

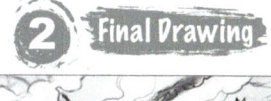

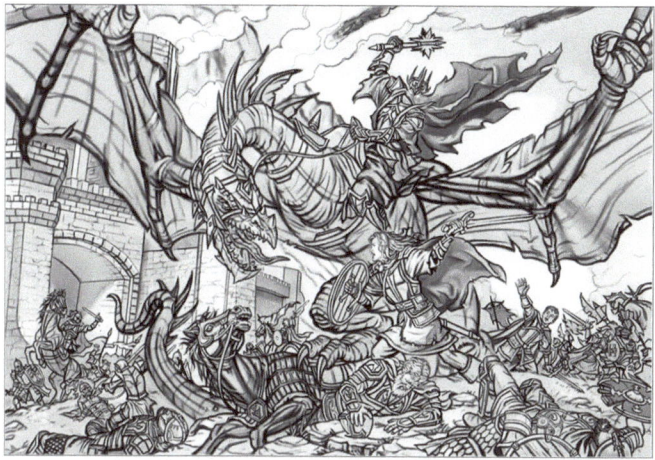

4 Work In Progress

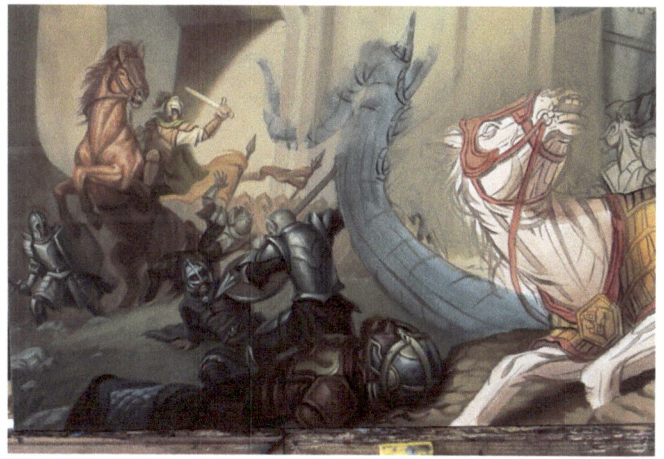

5 Detail Close-Ups

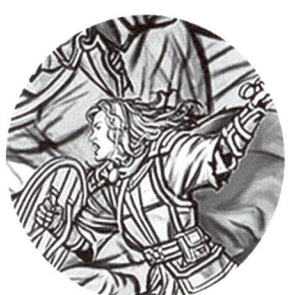
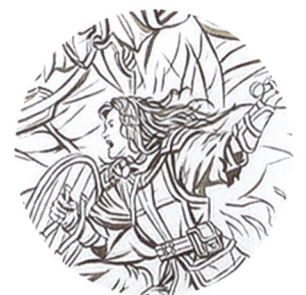
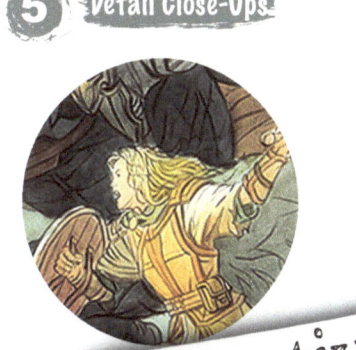
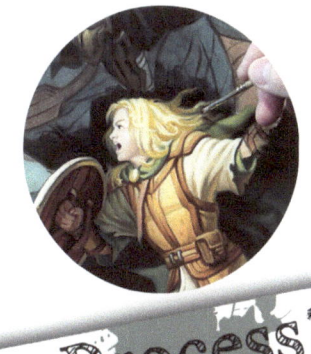

Creative Process

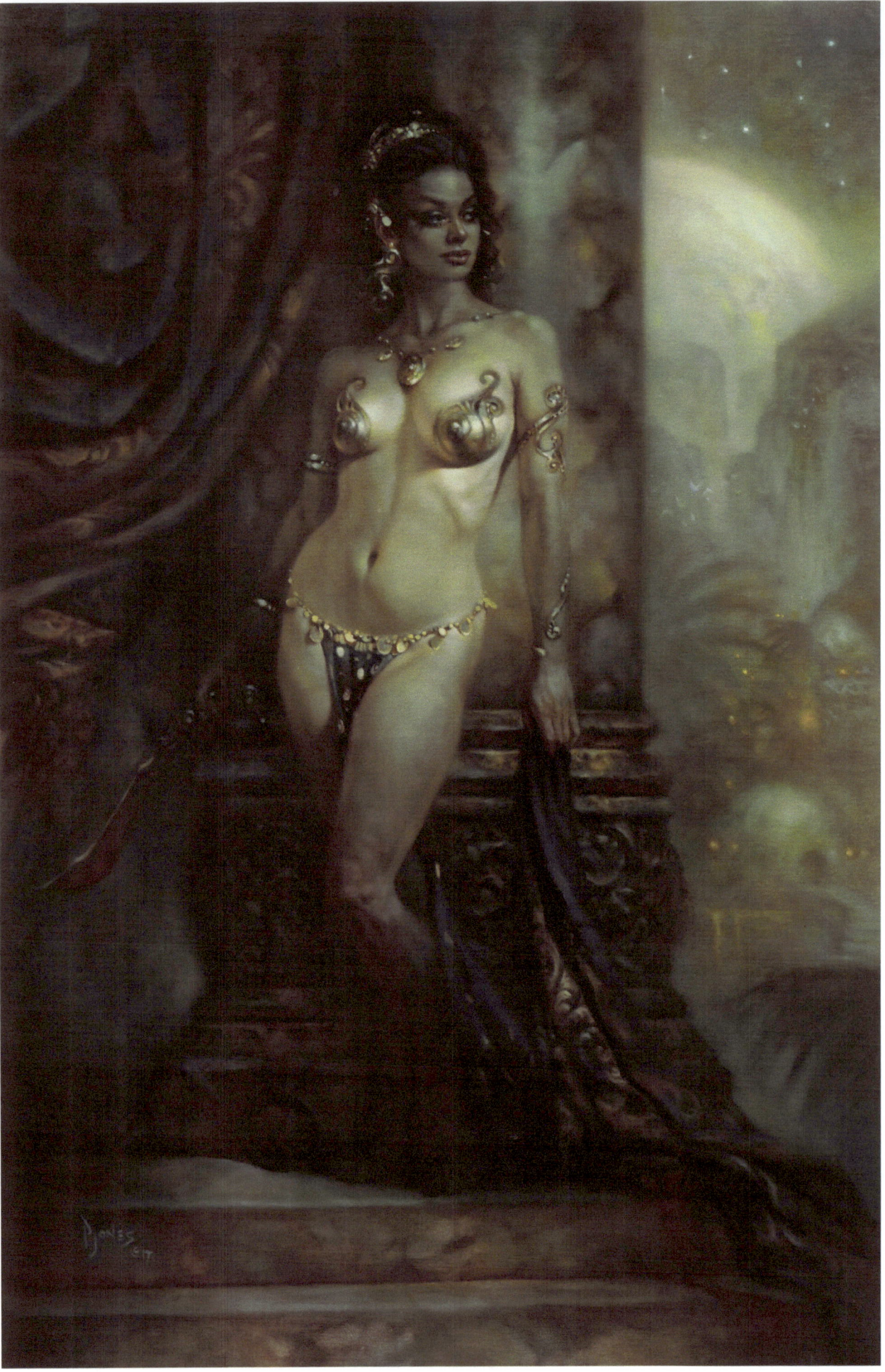

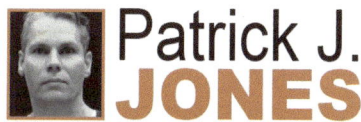

Patrick J. JONES
- www.pjartworks.com
- Blood Temple
- Oils on canvas 36"x 24"

1. Rough Sketches

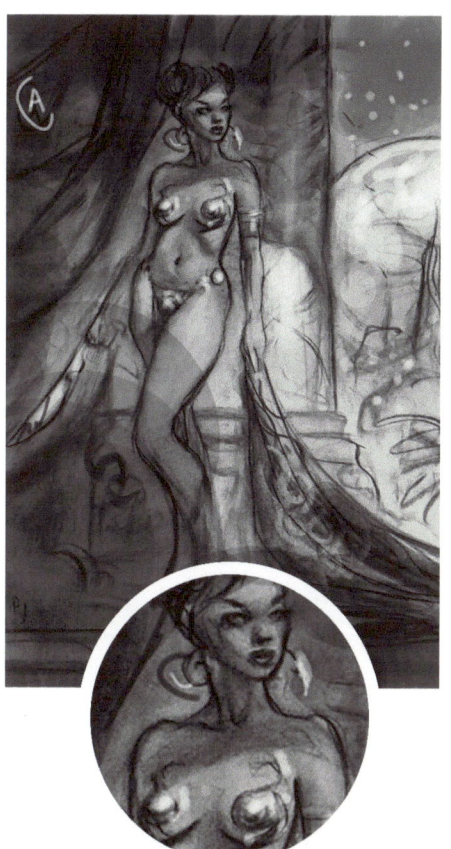
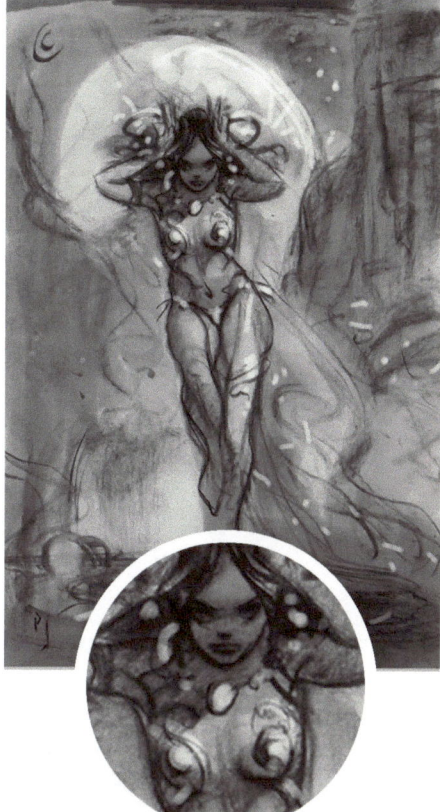
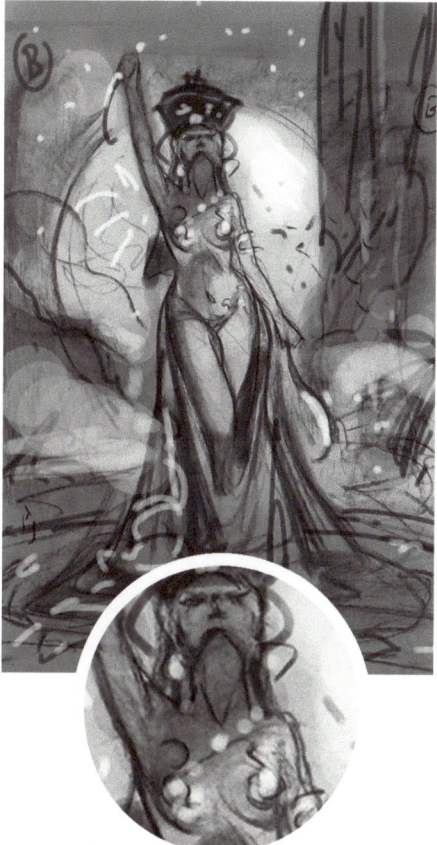

2. Color Rough

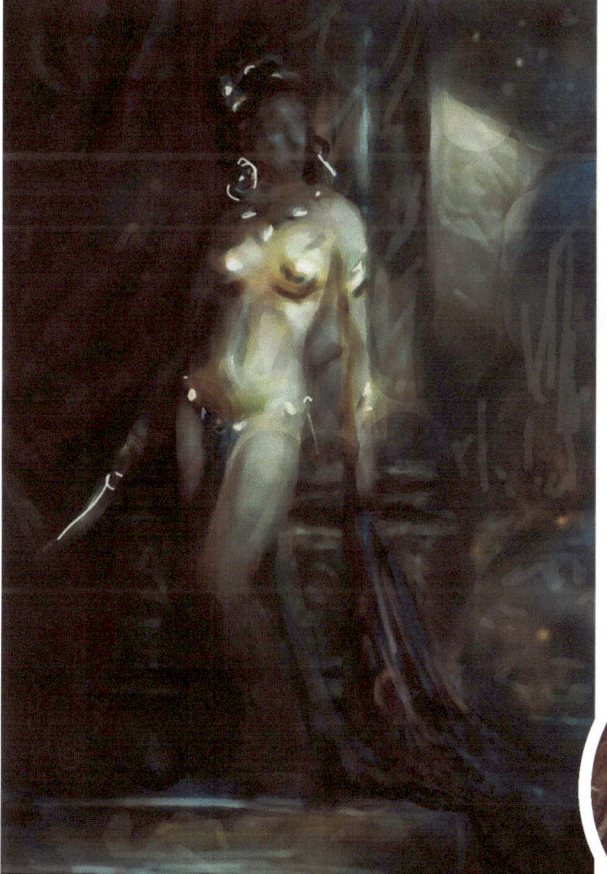

3. Detail Close-Ups

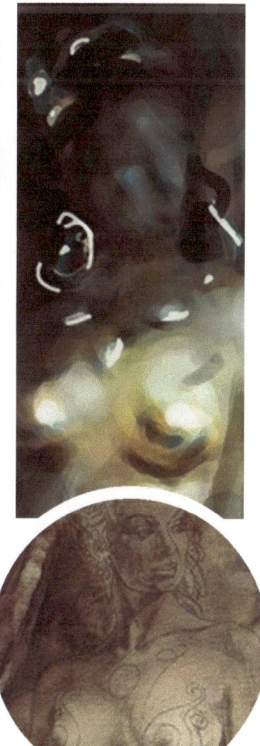

4. Underpainting

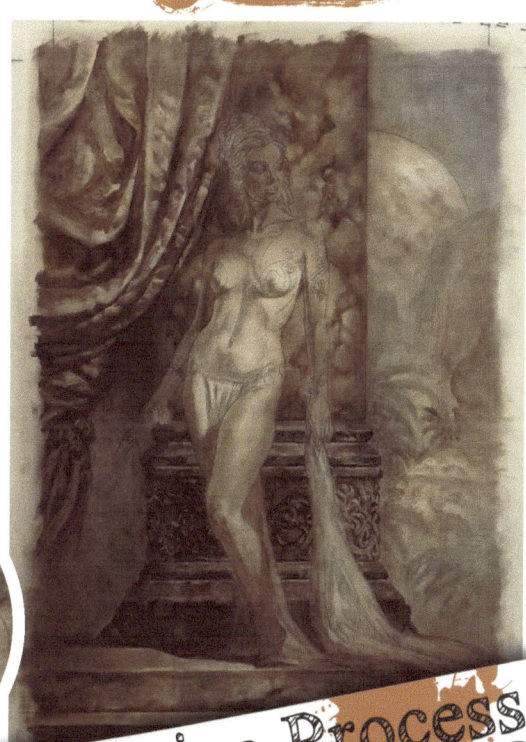

Creative Process — Vision Illustrated

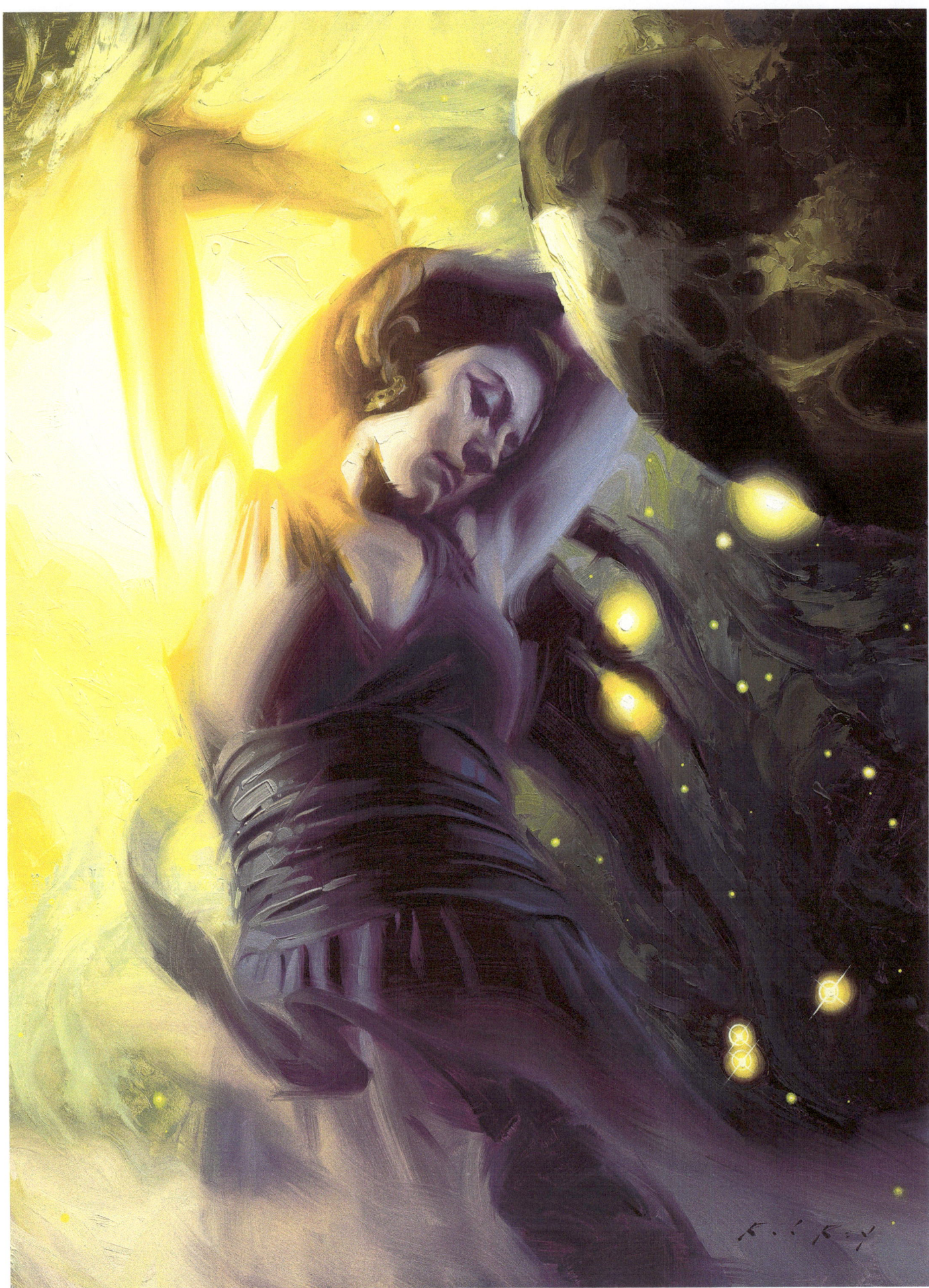

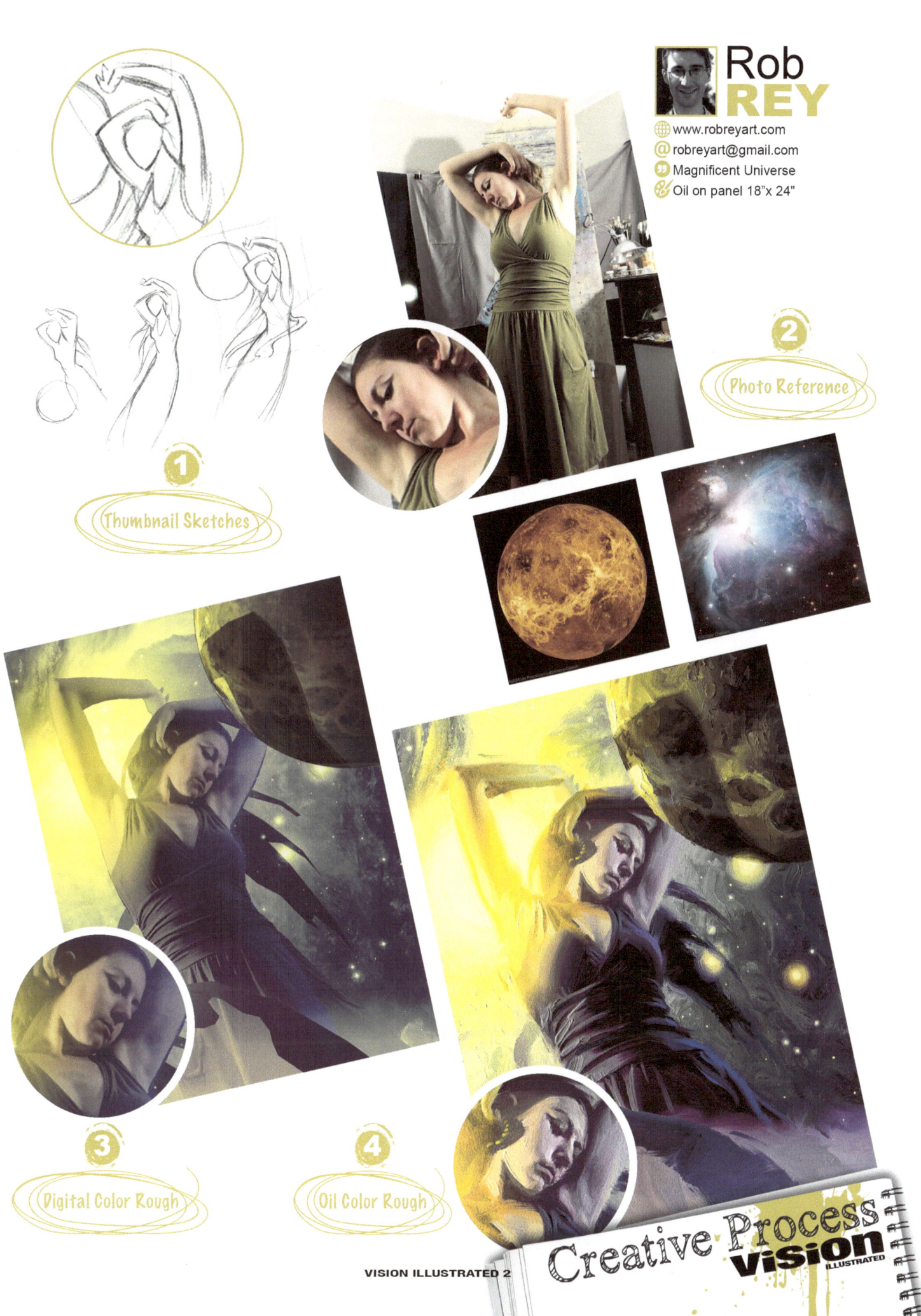

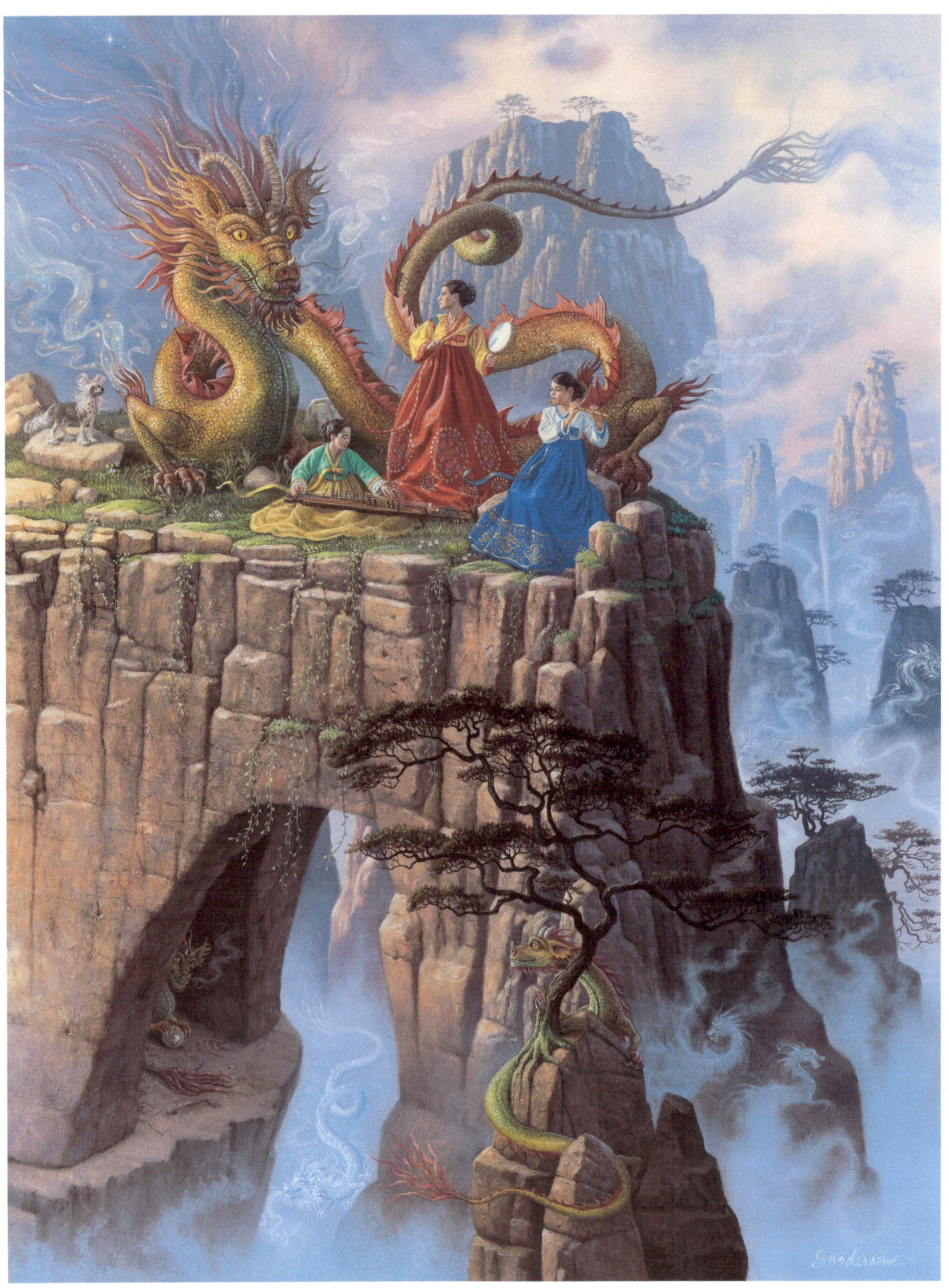

Ruth SANDERSON

- www.ruthsanderson.com
- ruth@ruthsanderson.com
- Dragon Serenade
- Oil on board 30"x 40"

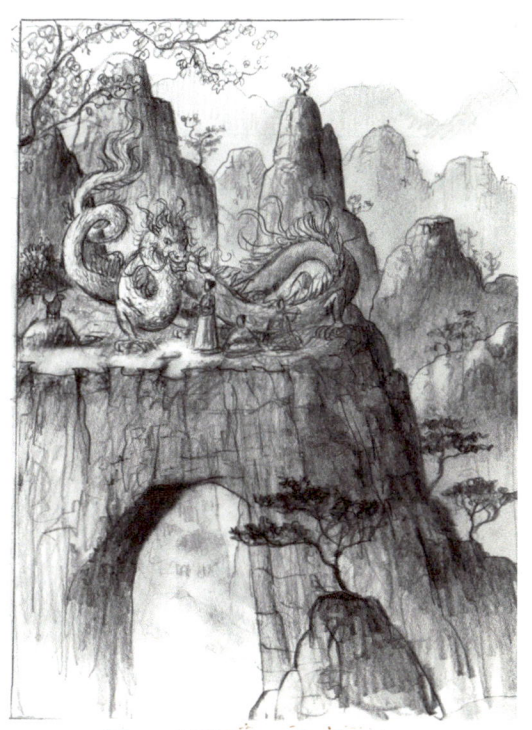

1 Thumbnail Sketch

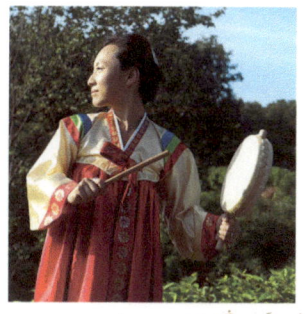
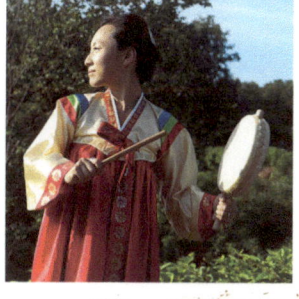
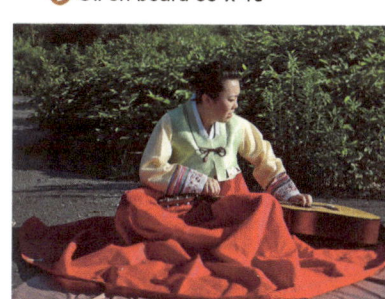
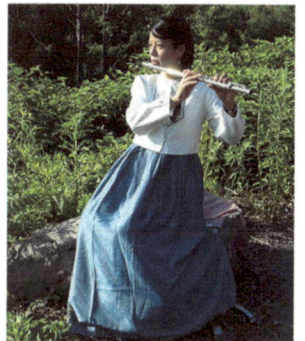

2 Photo Reference

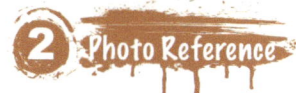

3 Sketch

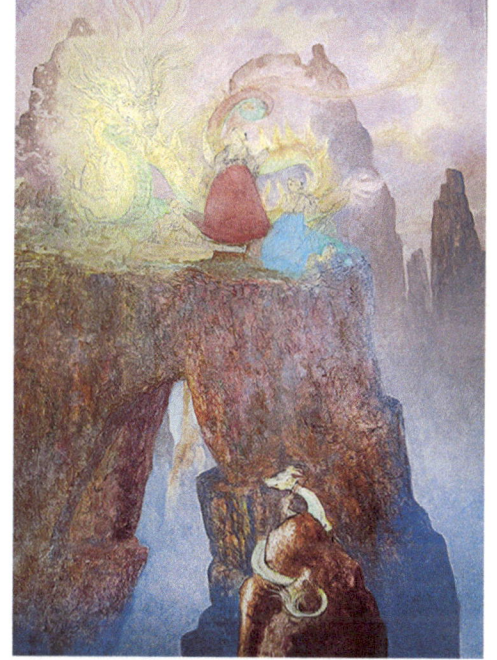

4 Underpainting

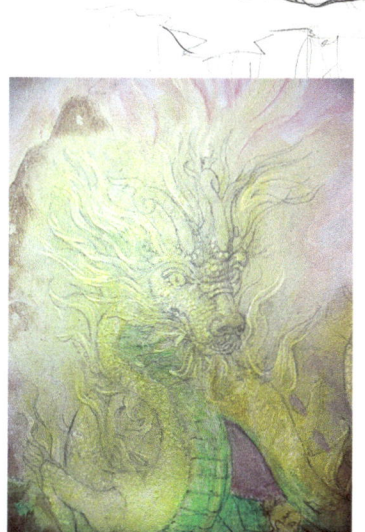
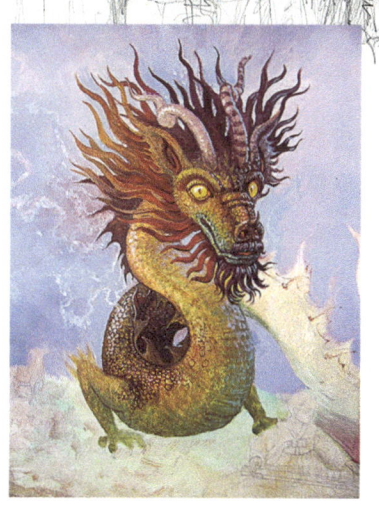
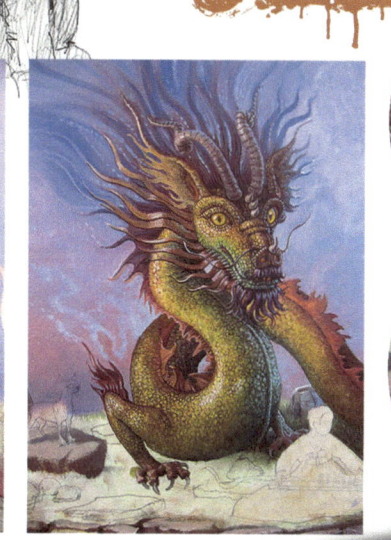
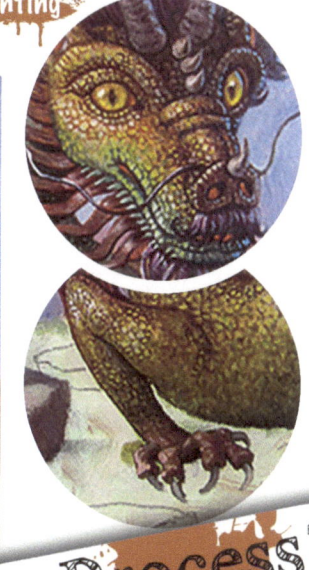

5 Work In Progress

Creative Process

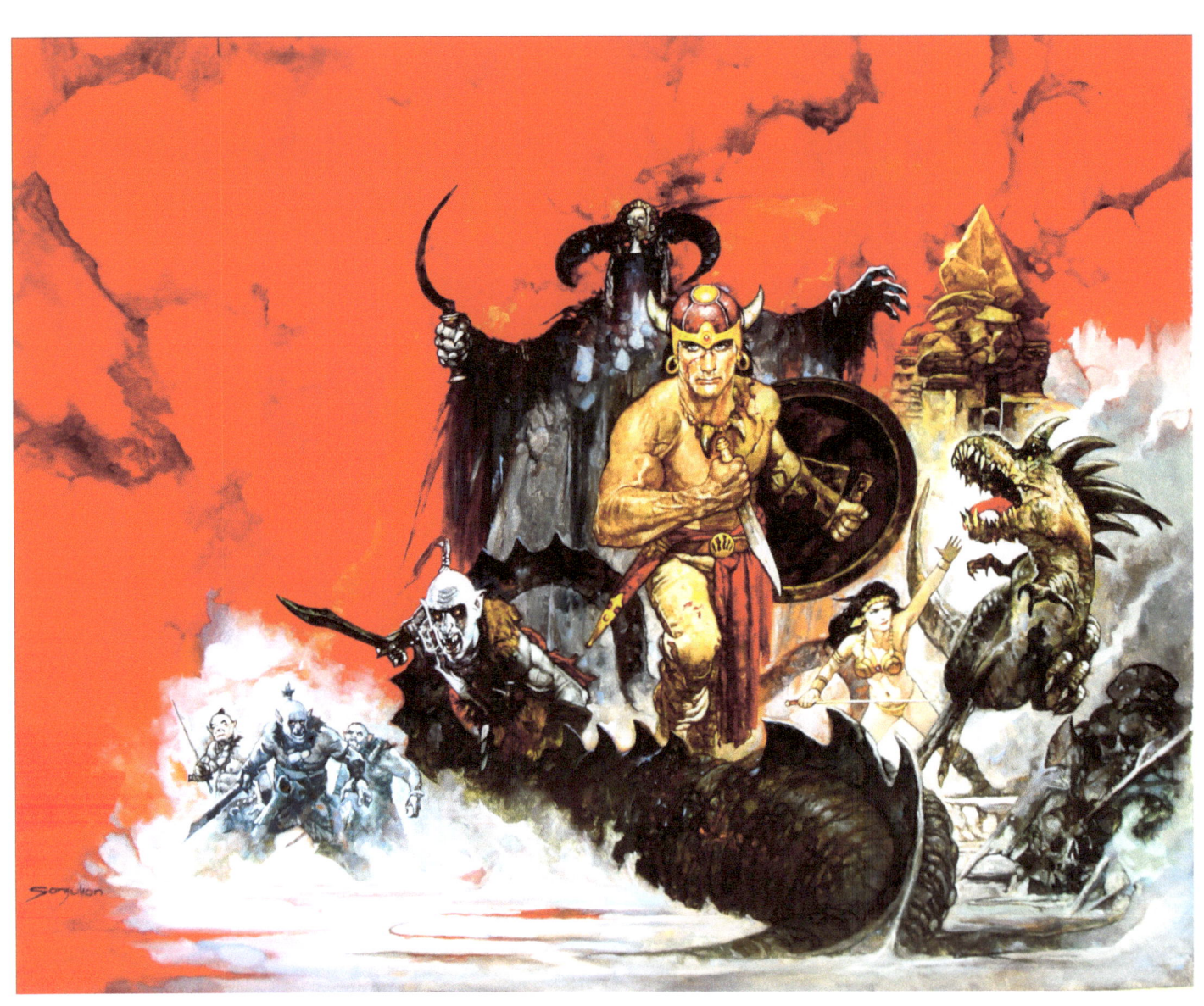

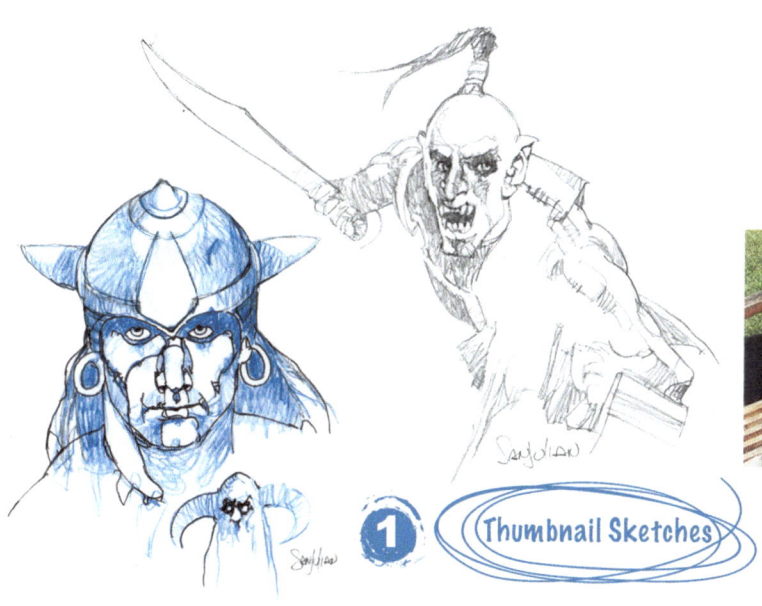
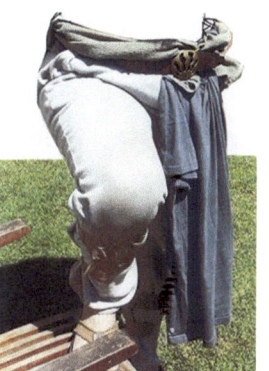

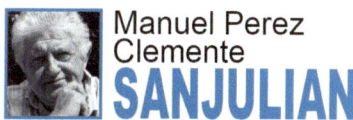
Manuel Perez Clemente
SANJULIAN
www.sanjulian.info
Conan Juego de Rol (libro)
Oil on canvas 28.5" x 35.5"

 Thumbnail Sketches

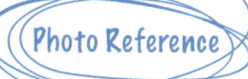 **Photo Reference**

 Final Sketch

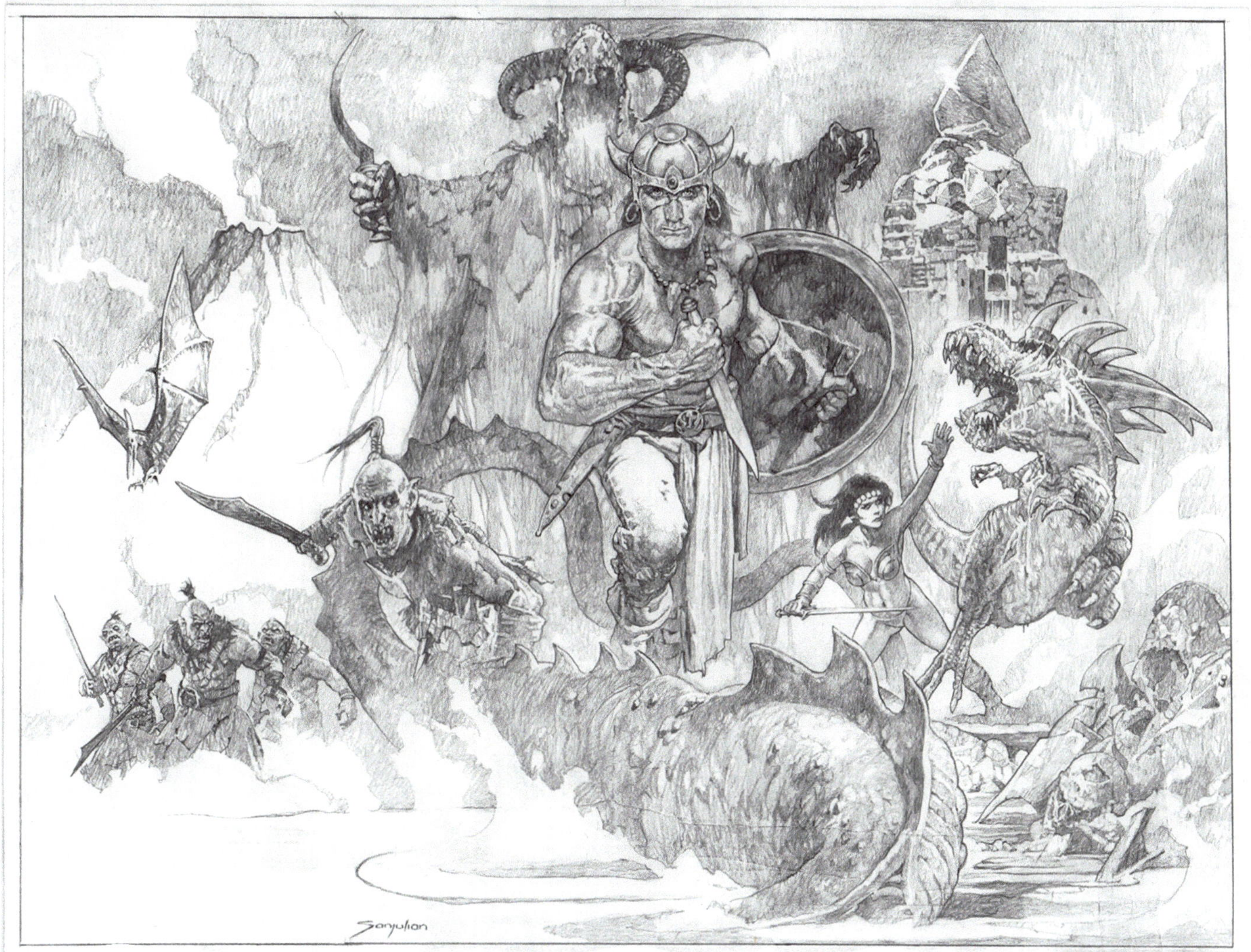

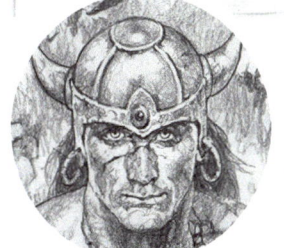 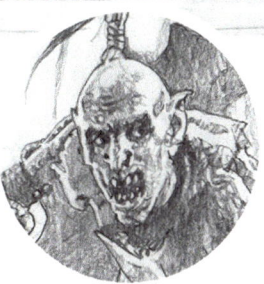 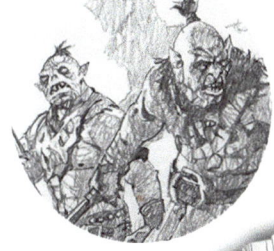 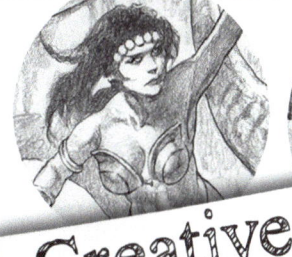 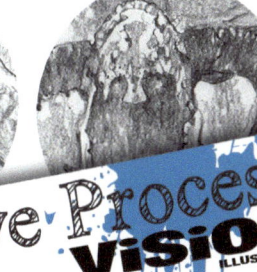

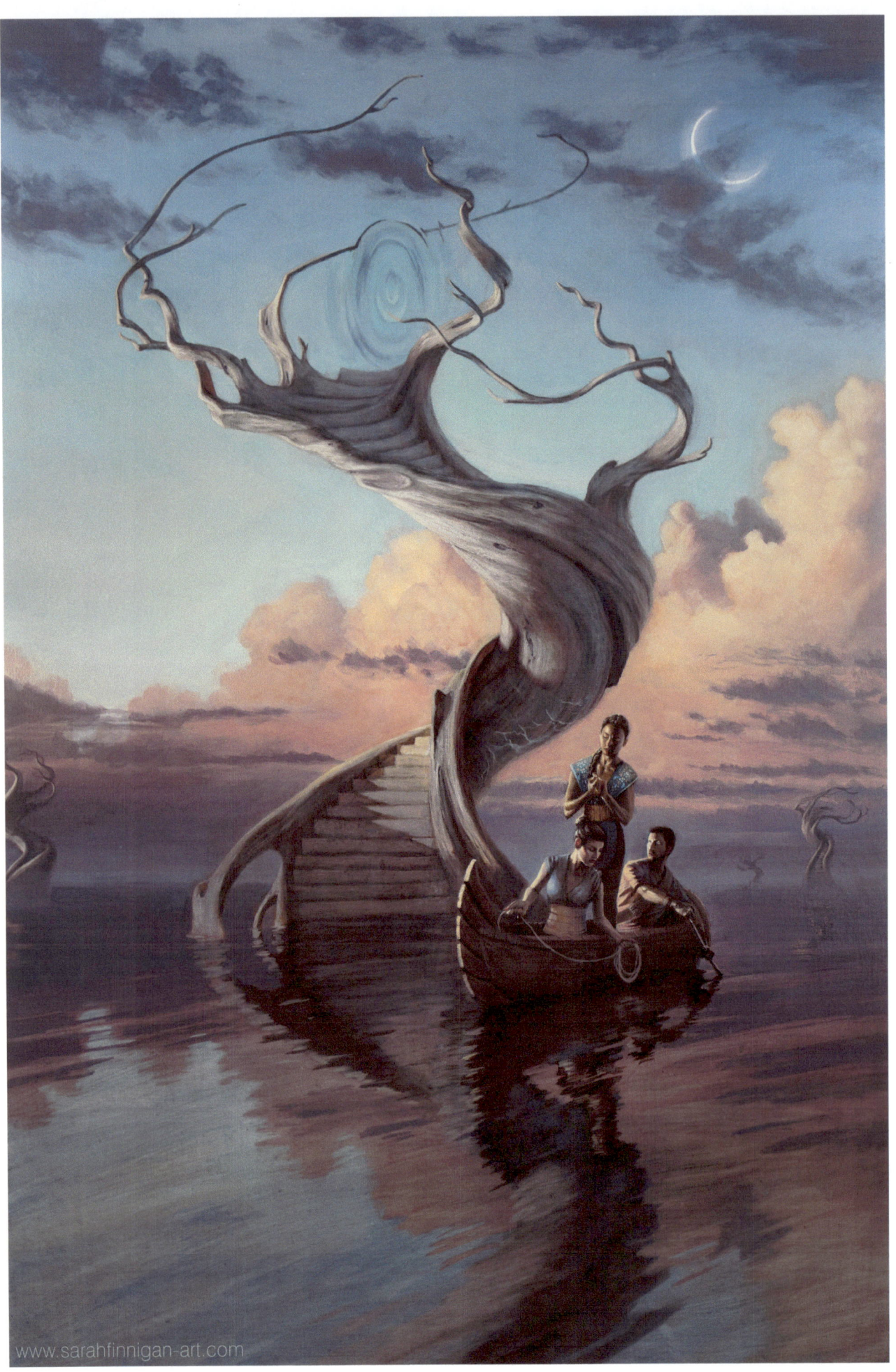

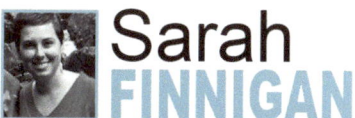

Sarah FINNIGAN

🌐 www.sarahfinnigan.com
@ sarahfinnigan.art@gmail.com
❞ The Way Between
✎ Acrylic on panel 19"x 28"

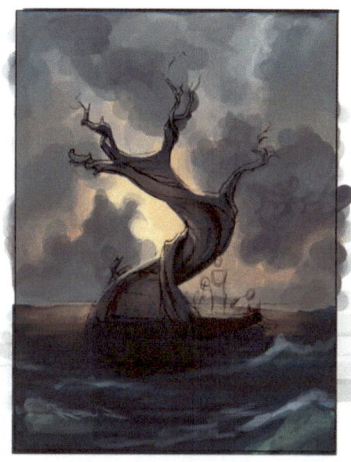
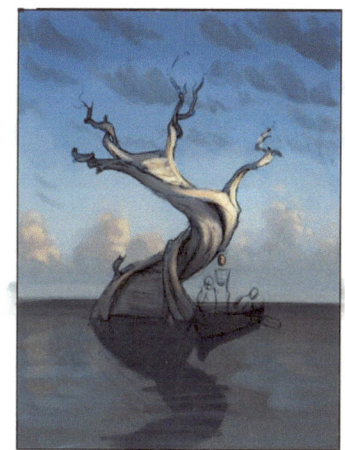
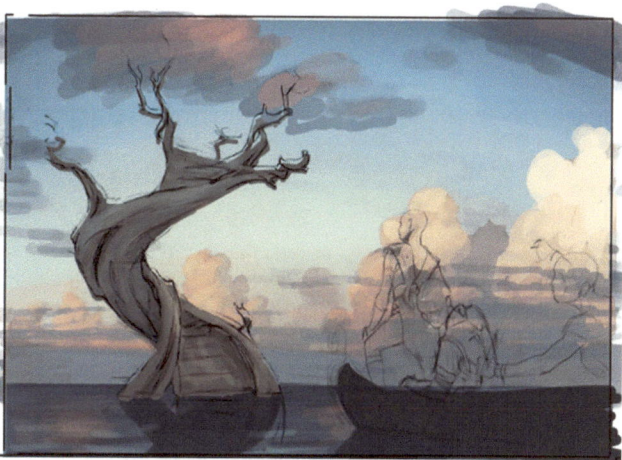
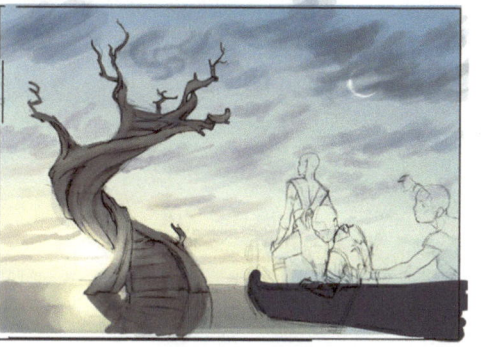

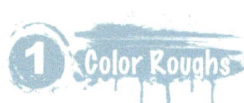
1 Color Roughs

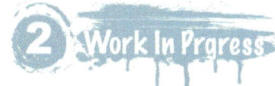
2 Work In Prgress

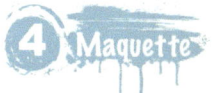
3 Detail Close-Ups

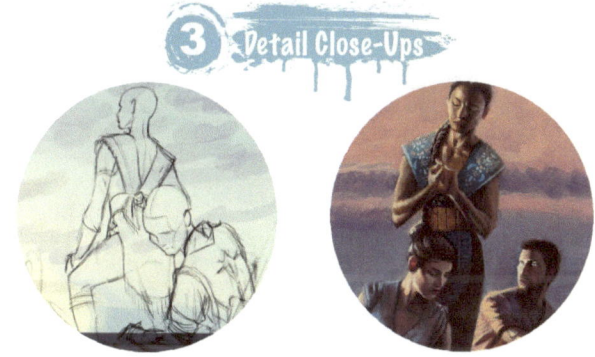

4 Maquette

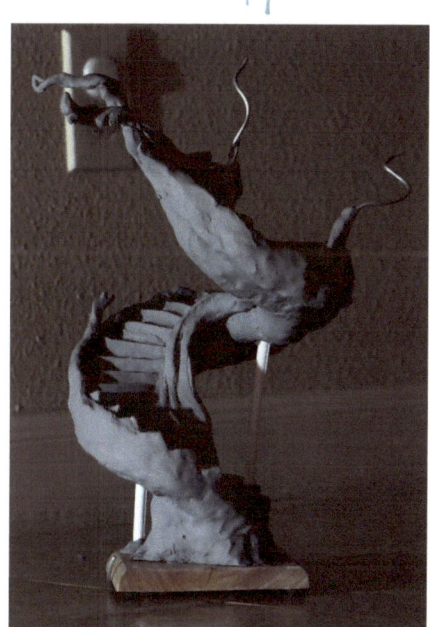
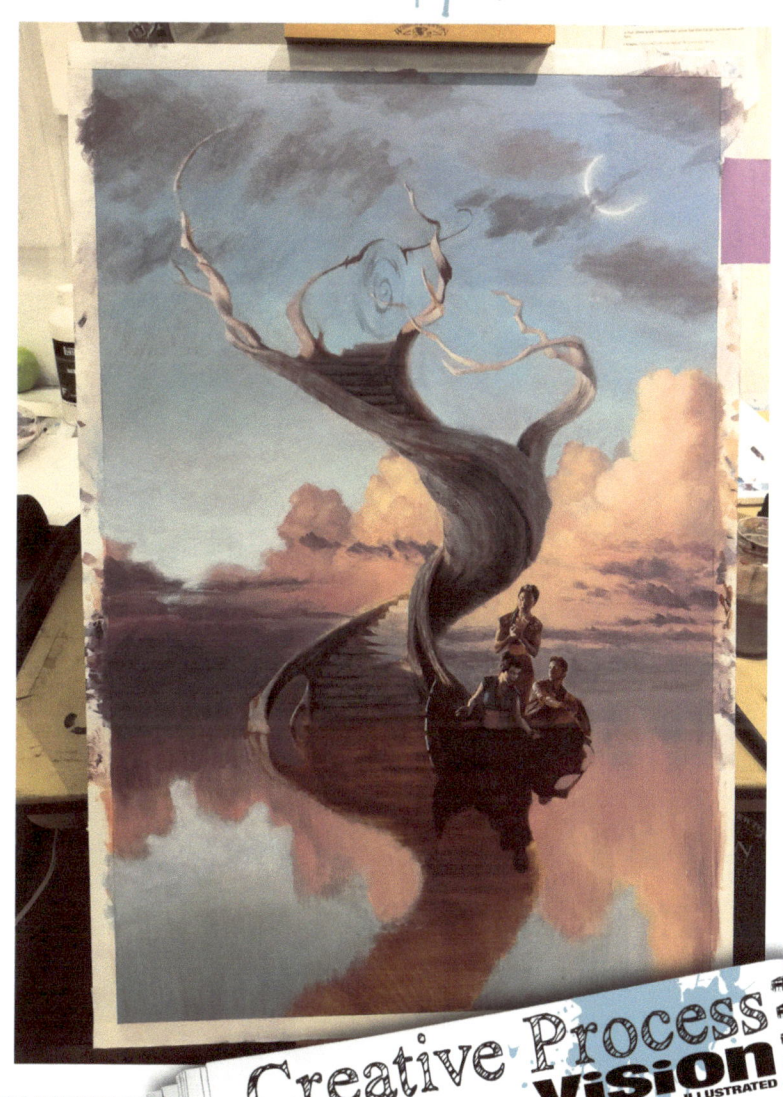

Creative Process
VISION ILLUSTRATED

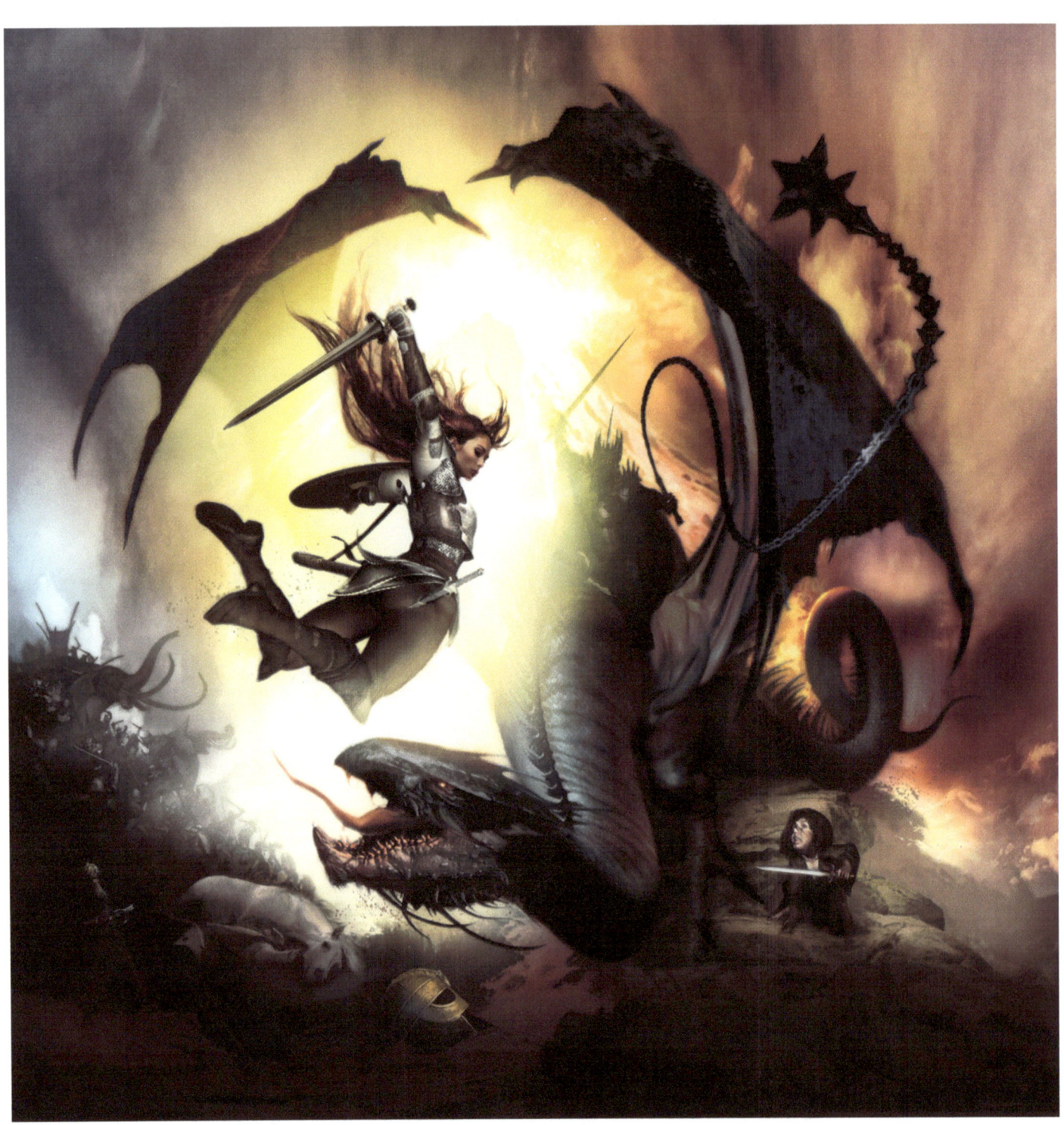

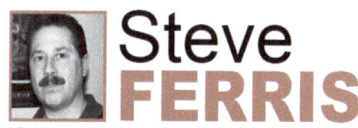

Steve FERRIS

🌐 www.steveferris.com
@ steveferris@optonline.net
💬 Eowyn
🖌 Pencil, Acrylic, Oil.
Mixed Media 19"x 28"

1 Rough Sketch

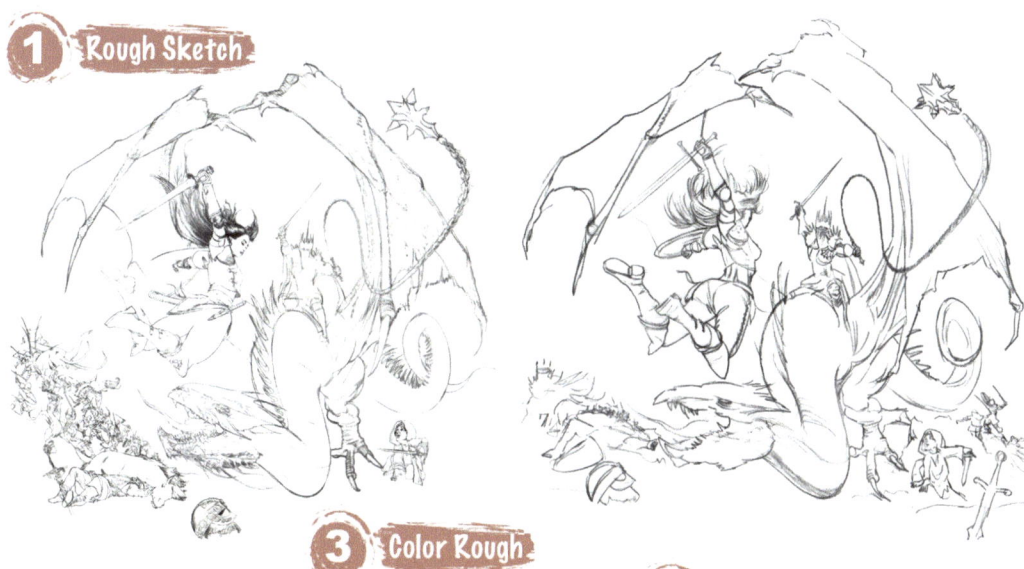

2 Final Sketch

3 Color Rough

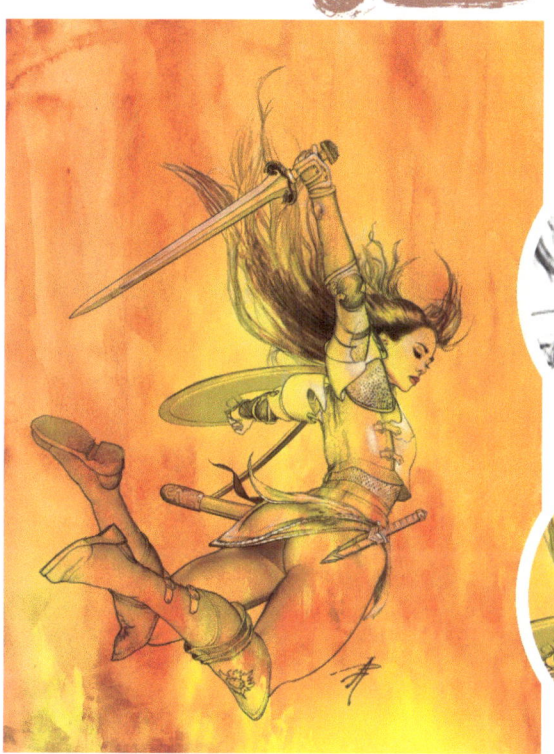

4 Detail Close-Ups

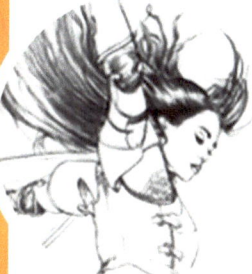
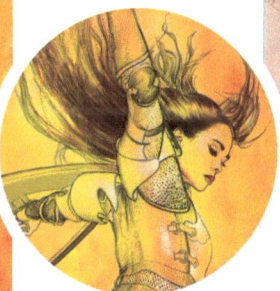

5 Underpainting

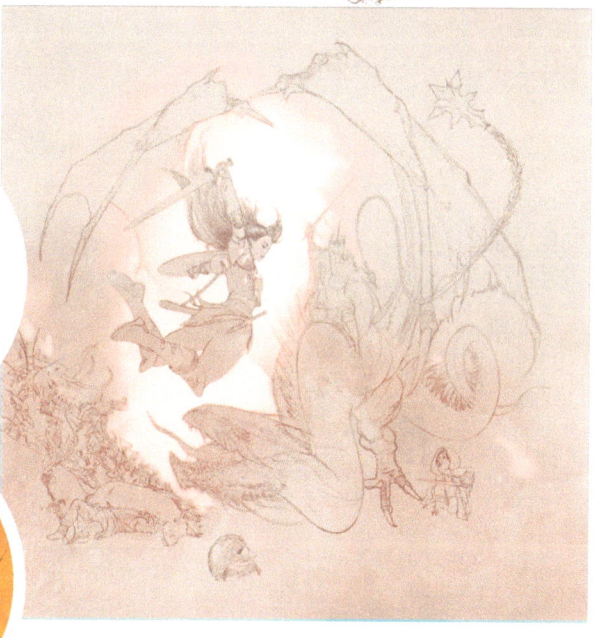

6 Work In Progress

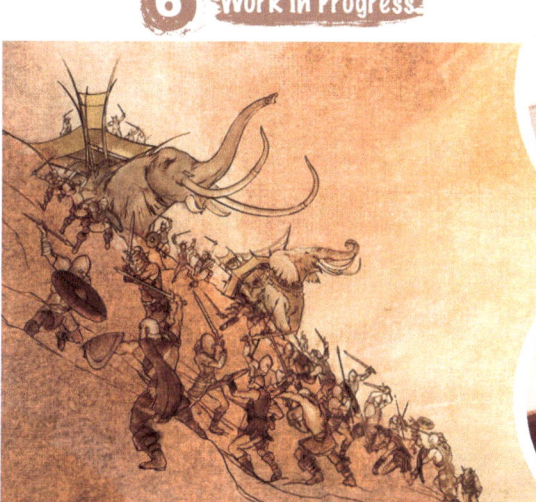

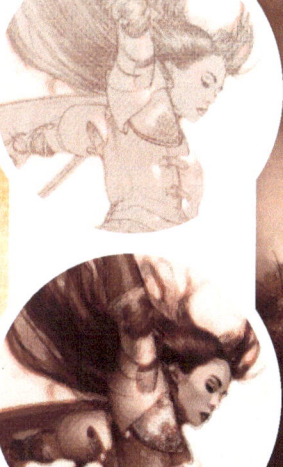
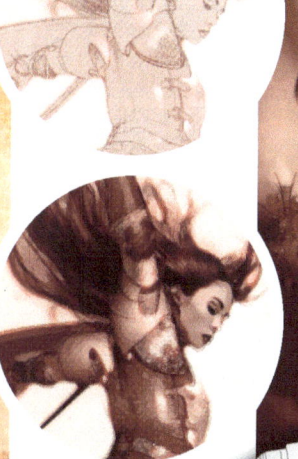

7 Underpainting

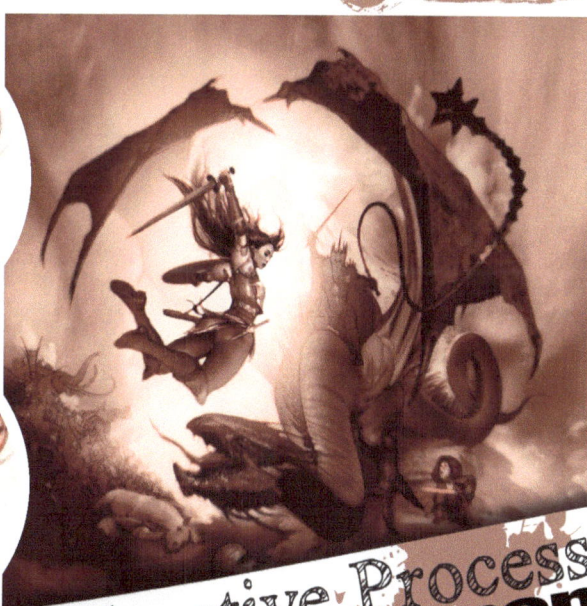

Creative Process — VISION ILLUSTRATED

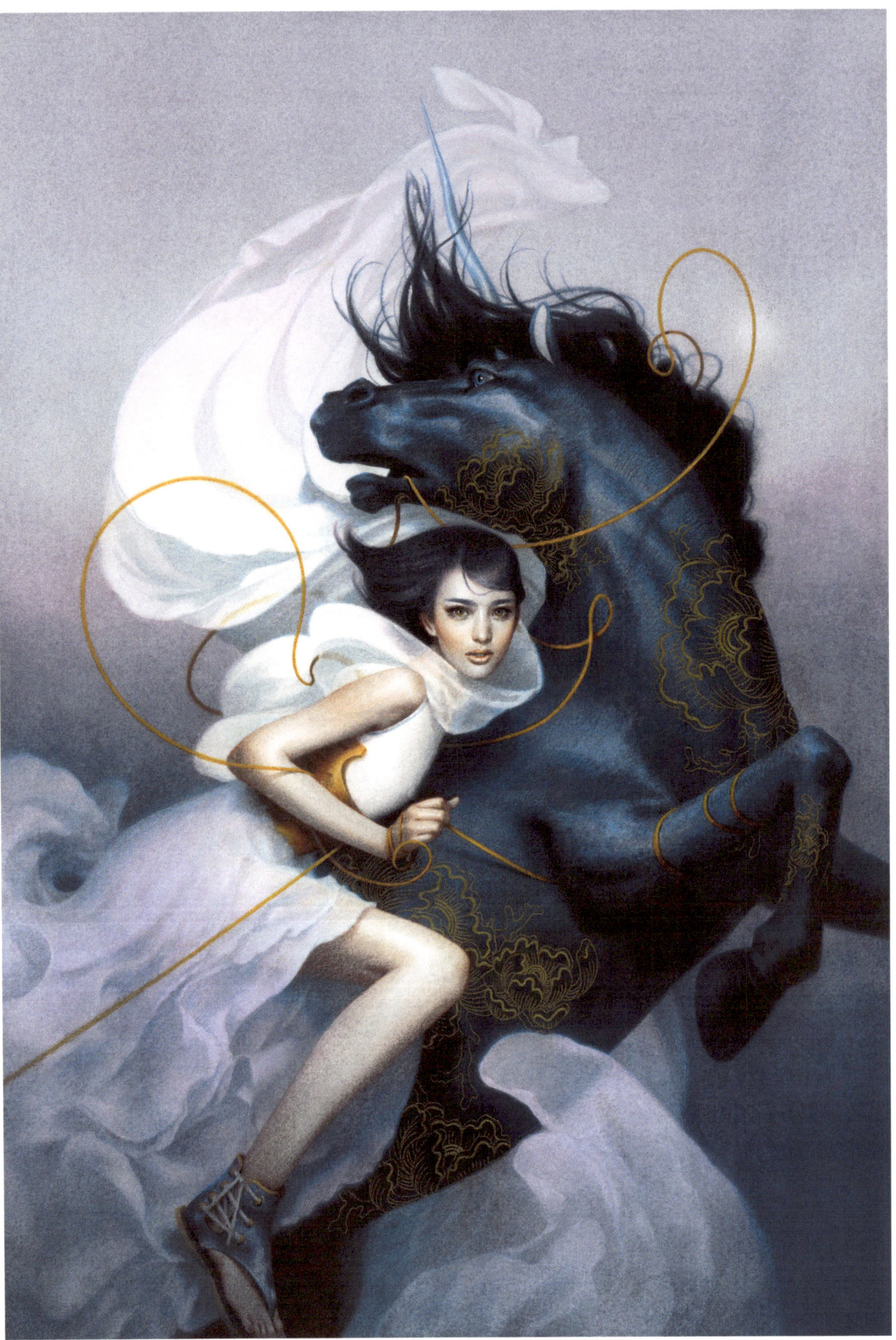

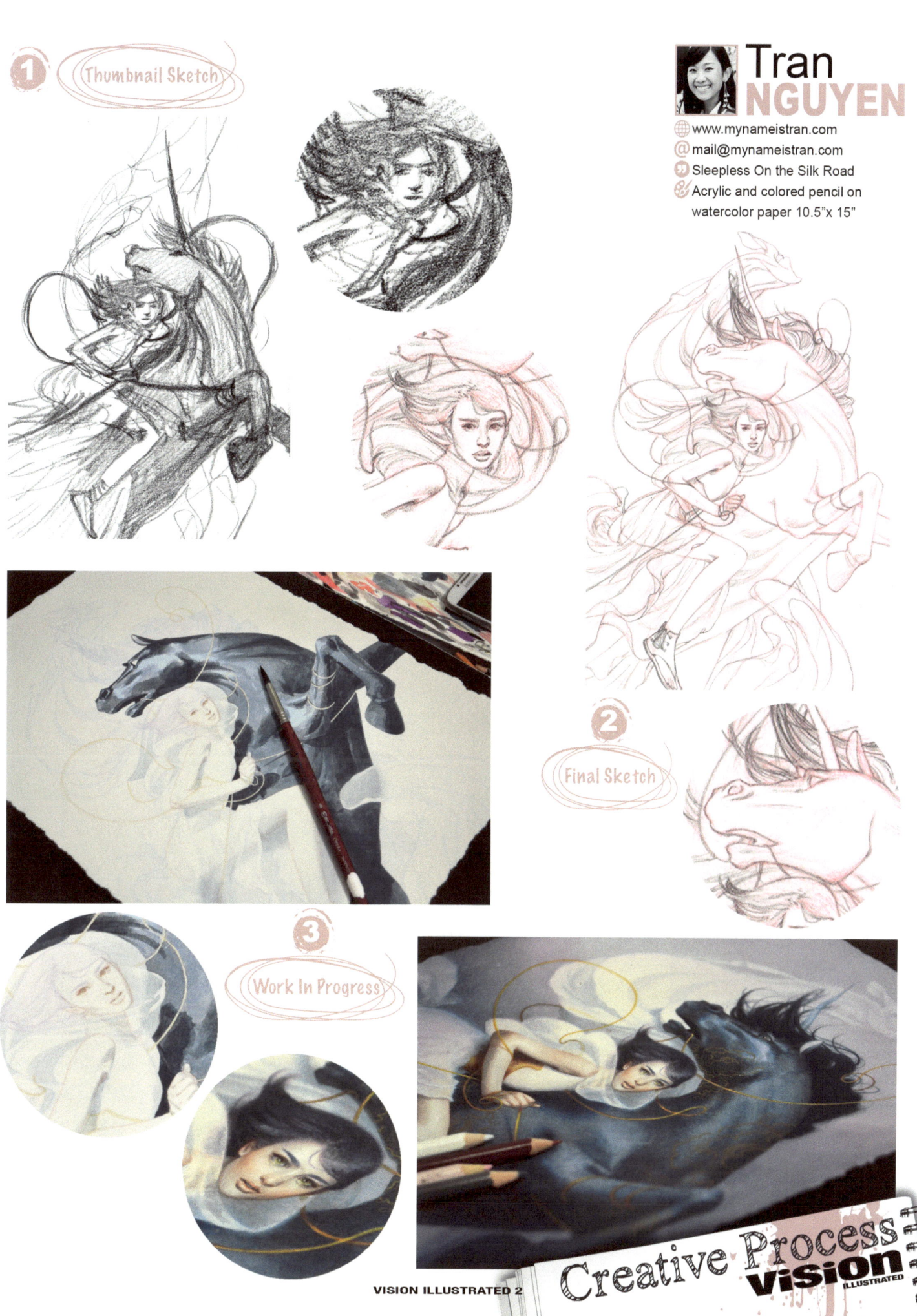

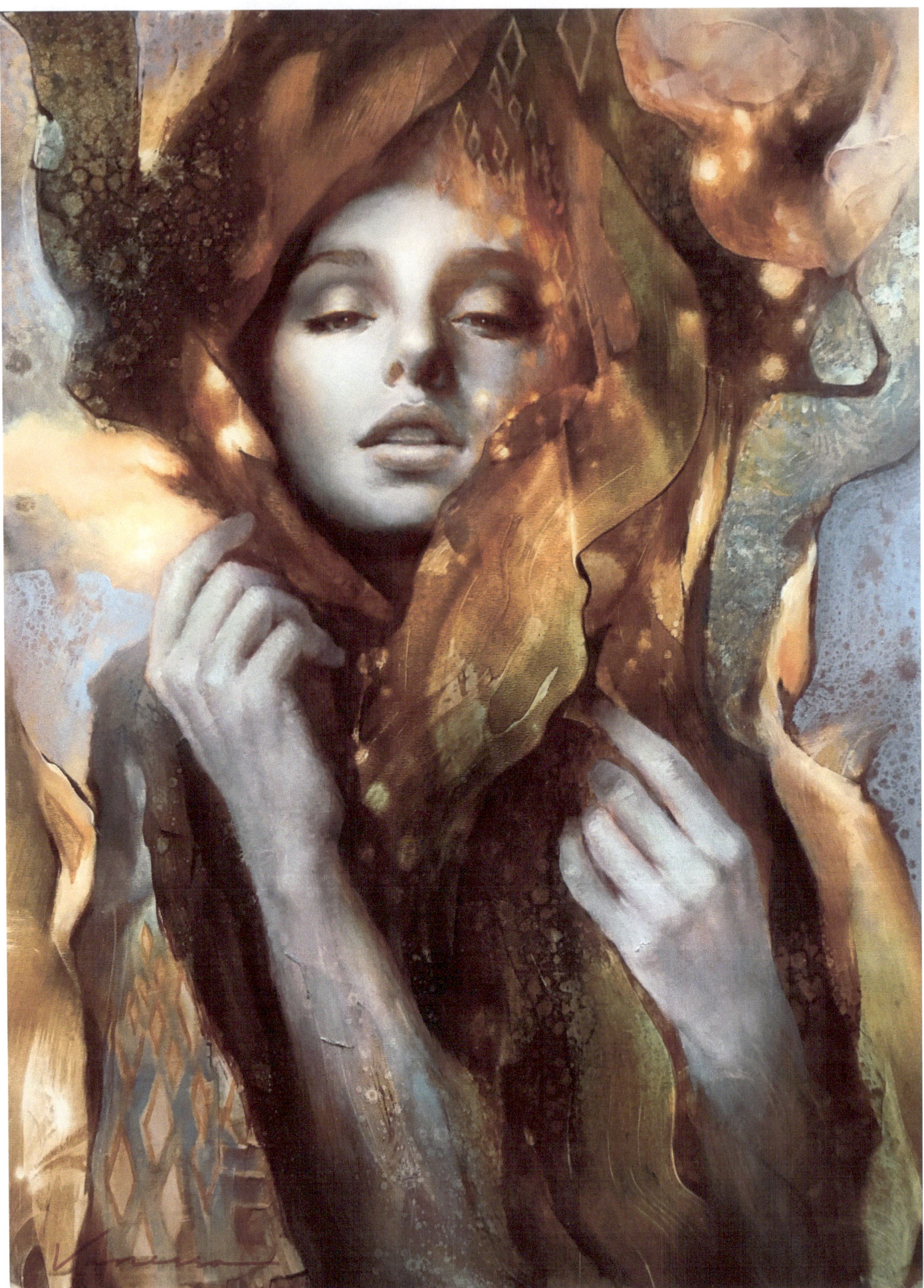

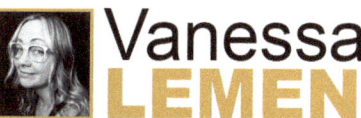
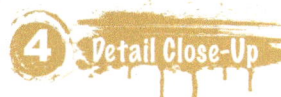

www.vanessalemenart.com
Gaia
Oil on panel 9"x 12"

4 Detail Close-Up

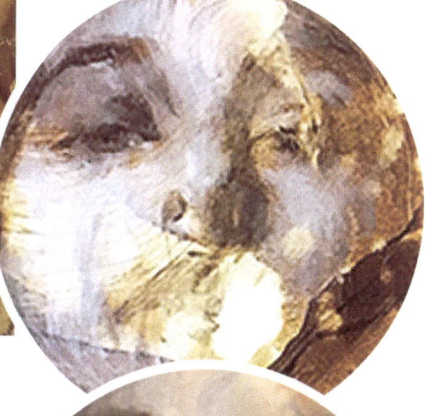
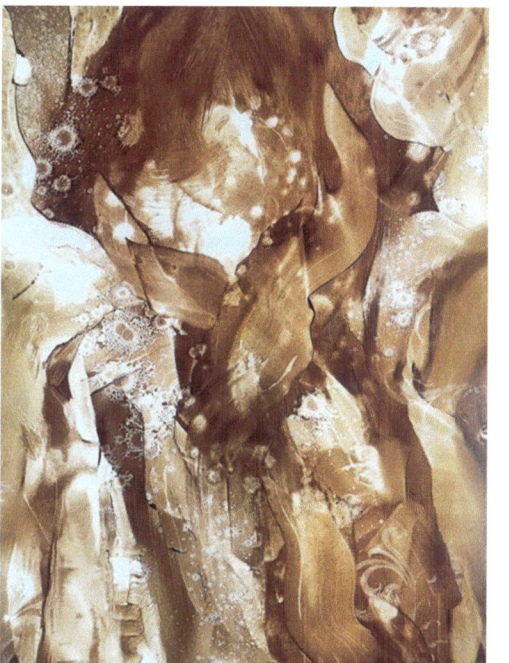
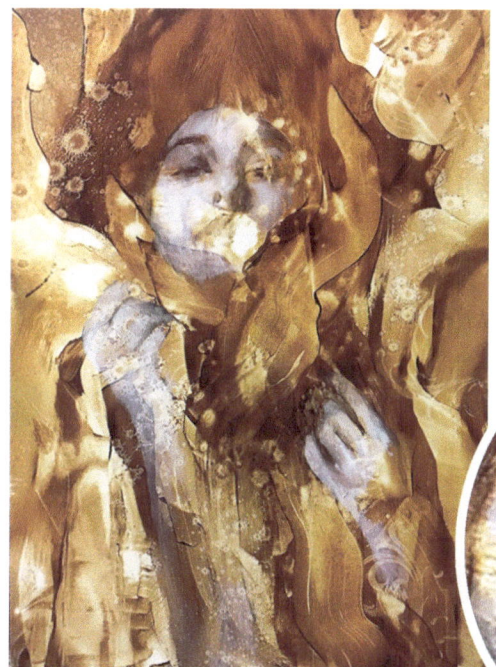

1 Work In Progress

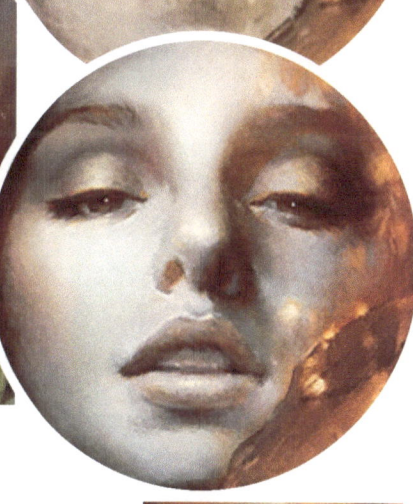
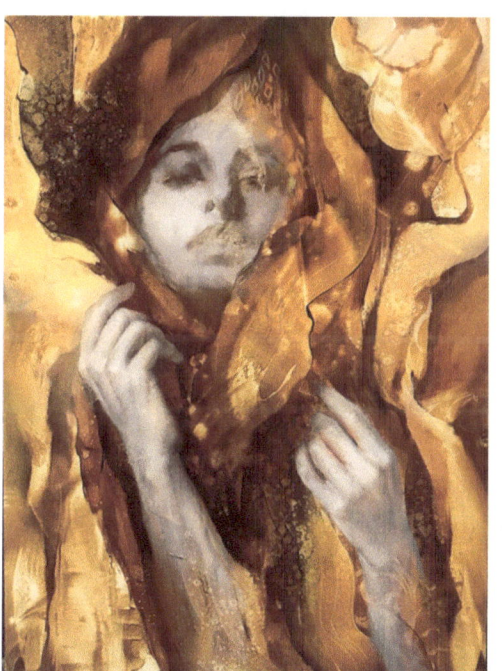
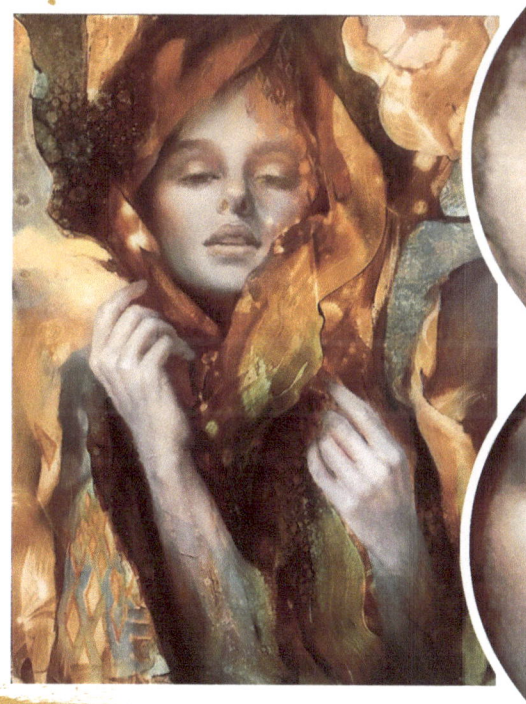

2 Work In Progress

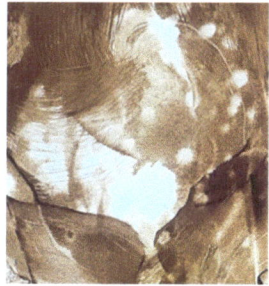
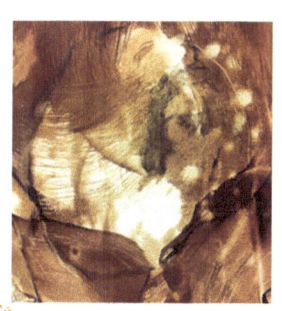
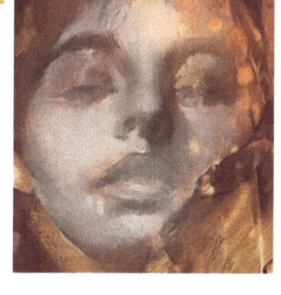
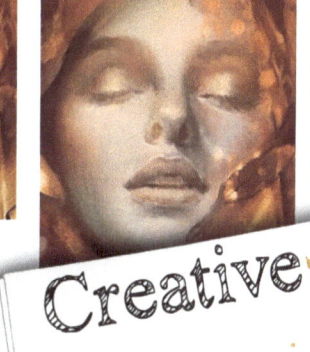
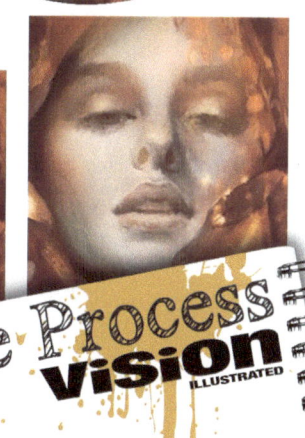

3 Work In Progress

VISION ILLUSTRATED 2

Creative Process VISION ILLUSTRATED

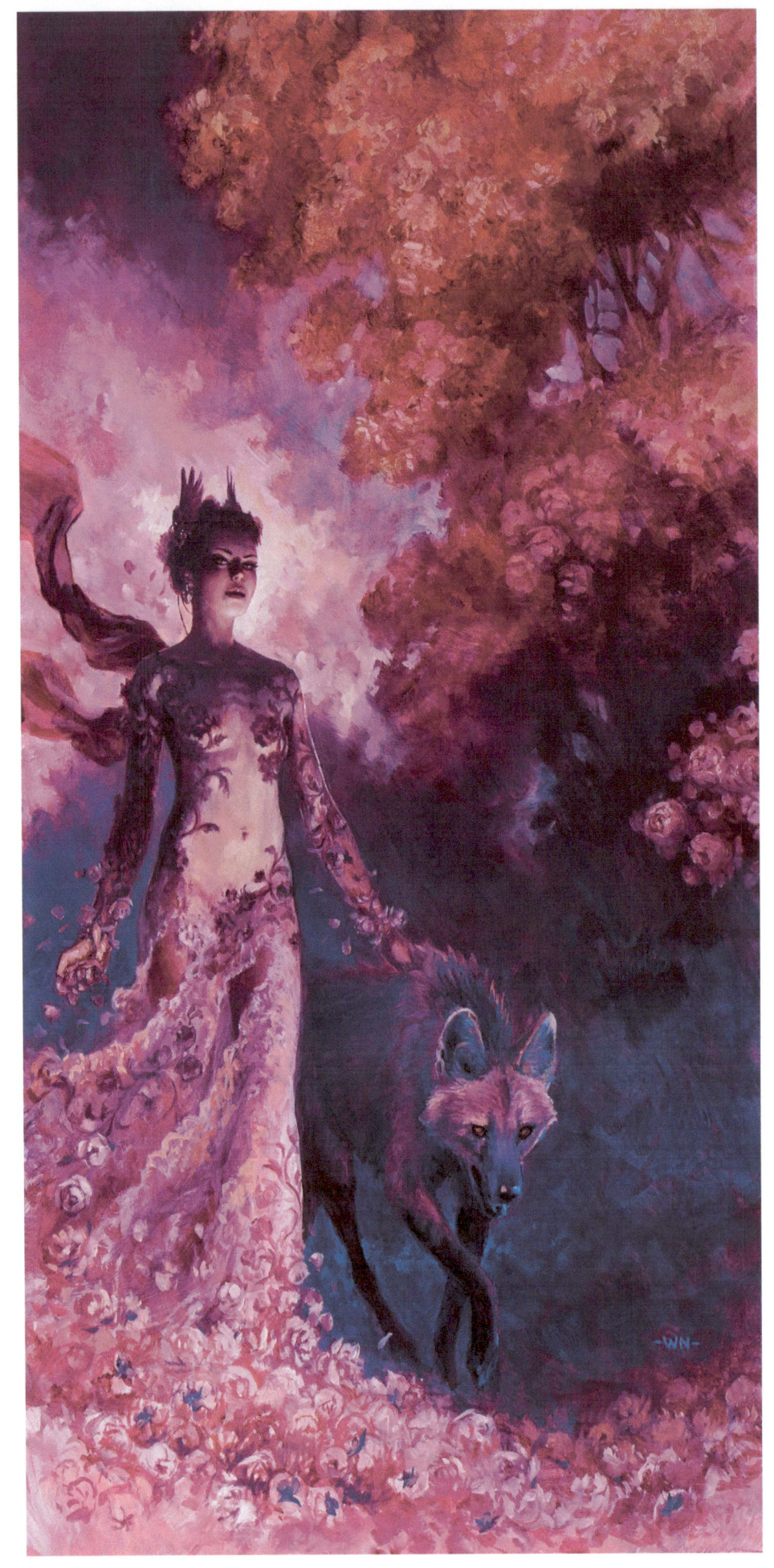

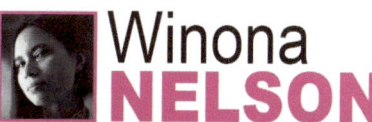

Winona NELSON

🌐 www.winonanelson.com
@ wnelsonart@gmail.com
💬 Bloom
🖌 Acrylic and oil on masonite 12"x24"

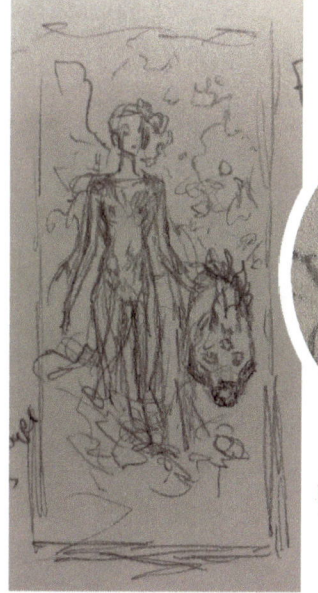
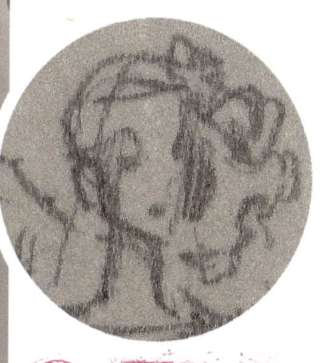
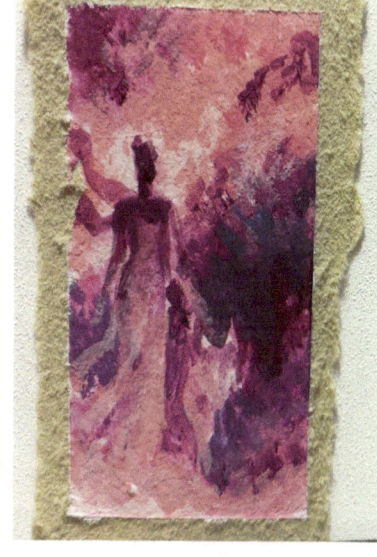
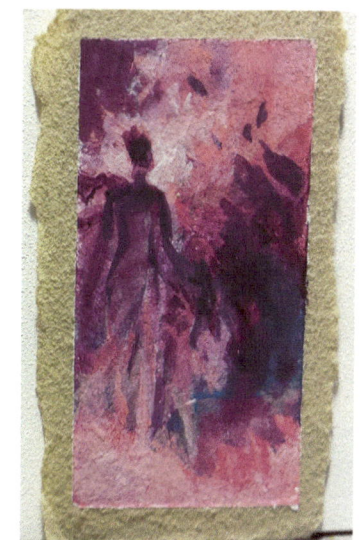

1 Work In Progress

2 Color Roughs

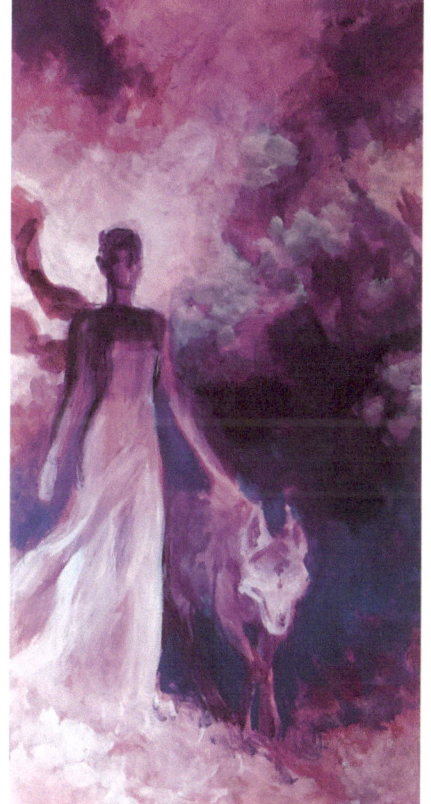
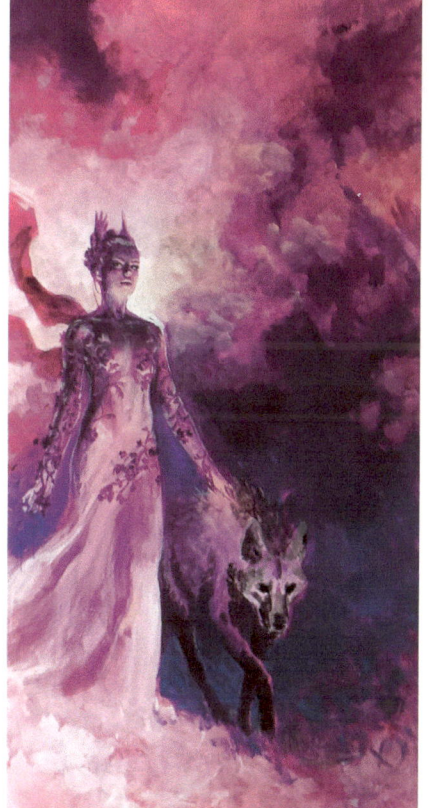
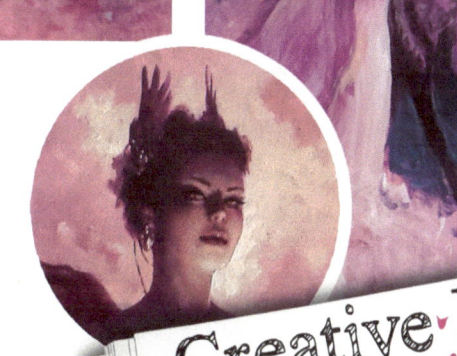

3 Work In Progress

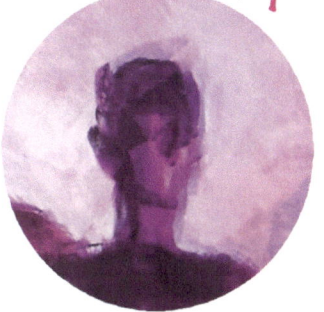
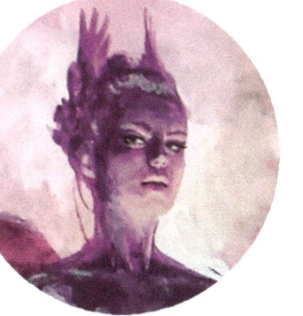
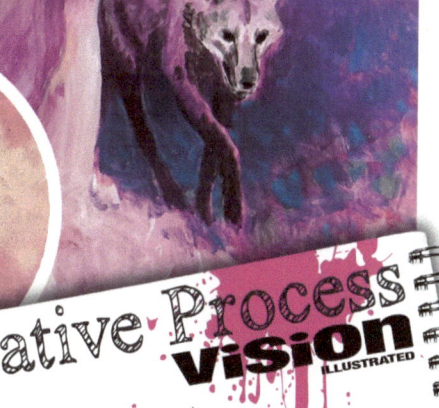

VISION ILLUSTRATED 2

Creative Process

Fantastic Art And The Creative Process

Volume 2

ViSiON
ILLUSTRATED